089397

1837

DM 11/06

D0120566

1581

COMMISSIONING AND PURCHASING

The mixed economy of welfare is a reality in social care. The rise of the independent sector has been mirrored by a shift in emphasis in the role of government. Commissioning services has become a dominant role for the public services yet it is an area which has received little attention. This book, written by a senior manager, looks at the skills needed to translate the concept of commissioning into cost-effective and high quality services.

After explaining how the social care world changed dramatically in the 1990s, Terry Bamford explains the difference between commissioning and purchasing. Using a wealth of case studies and activities, he shows how to involve service users in the process, how to write contracts, and how to get value for money.

Commissioning and Purchasing is a practical handbook. It will be invaluable to those undertaking commissioning tasks from the frontline worker to the senior manager or to the social care student in training. No one will read this book without having a better idea of how to get the best possible service at the most reasonable cost, nor will they have any illusions about the complexity of the task.

Terry Bamford spent fifteen years heading social services, most recently as Executive Director of Housing and Social Services in Kensington and Chelsea. A former Chair of the British Association of Social Workers, he has written extensively on social care issues.

the social work skills series

published in association with *Community Care*

series editor: Terry Philpot

the social work skills series

- builds practice skills step by step
- places practice in its policy context
- relates practice to relevant research
- provides a secure base for professional development

This new, skills-based series has been developed by Routledge and *Community Care* working together in partnership to meet the changing needs of today's students and practitioners in the broad field of social care. Written by experienced practitioners and teachers with a commitment to passing on their knowledge to the next generation, each text in the series features: *learning objectives*; *case examples*; *activities to test knowledge and understanding*; *summaries of key learning points*; *key references*; *suggestions for further reading*.

Also available in the series:

Tackling Social Exclusion
John Pierson
Institute of Social Work and Applied Social Studies, Staffordshire University

Managing Aggression
Ray Braithwaite
Consultant and trainer in managing aggression at work. Lead trainer and speaker in the national 'No Fear' campaign.

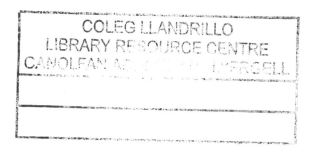
COLEG LLANDRILLO
LIBRARY RESOURCE CENTRE
CANOLFAN ADNODDAU LLYFRGELL

COMMISSIONING AND PURCHASING

Terry Bamford

communitycare

London and New York

COLEG LLANDRILLO
LIBRARY RESOURCE CENTRE
CANOLFAN ADNODDAU LLYFRGELL

11/06

089397   362 BAM

First published 2001
by Routledge
11 New Fetter Lane, London EC4P 4EE

Simultaneously published in the USA and Canada
by Routledge
29 West 35th Street, New York, NY 10001

Routledge is an imprint of the Taylor & Francis Group

© 2001 Terry Bamford

Designed and Typeset in Sabon and Futura by Keystroke,
Jacaranda Lodge, Wolverhampton
Printed and bound in Great Britain by
T J International Ltd, Padstow, Cornwall

All rights reserved. No part of this book may be reprinted or
reproduced or utilised in any form or by any electronic, mechanical,
or other means, now known or hereafter invented, including
photocopying and recording, or in any information storage or
retrieval system, without permission in writing from the publishers.

British Library Cataloguing in Publication Data
A catalogue record for this book is available from the British Library

Library of Congress Cataloging in Publication Data
Bamford Terry.
Commissioning and purchasing / Terry Bamford.
p.   cm. – (Social work skills series ; 2)
Published simultaneously in the USA and Canada.
Includes bibliographical references and index.
1. Social service–Contracting out–Great Britain. 2. Human services–Contracting out–
Great Britain. I. Series
HV245 .B33 2001
361.94–dc21   2001019966

ISBN 0–415–24742–X (hbk)
ISBN 0–415–24743–8 (pbk)

CONTENTS

FIGURES AND TABLES

FIGURES

TABLES

CASE STUDIES

CASE STUDIES

ACKNOWLEDGEMENTS

Writing books is a lonely endeavour. It opens up a dreadful self-doubt. Why should anybody be interested in one's views? Is there anything new to say? At these times the support of family, friends and colleagues is most helpful in keeping up the morale of the author. They probably did not know just how important to me was their interest in the progress of the book.

Retirement from full-time employment gave me the time to complete the work, but I am indebted to the many colleagues in Kensington and Chelsea and before that in the Southern Health and Social Services Board in Northern Ireland who have helped to shape the ideas discussed in the book. Particular thanks go to John Conway, John Jeremy and Mike O'Donnell who read the chapters on contracting and costs and prices respectively and offered advice. Marianne Griffiths kindly read the chapter on commissioning and offered helpful suggestions to improve the text. Any errors which remain would have been more grievous without their assistance, for which I am extremely grateful.

Terry Philpot has offered gentle encouragement as has Edwina Welham from Routledge. Their confidence that the book would be produced on time was a reassurance even when I was less certain.

I am grateful to the British Association of Social Workers, Gower Publishing Company, Jessica Kingsley Publications, the *Journal of Inter-Professional Care*, Lisieux Hall Publications, Macmillan Press, Open University Publications, Radcliffe Medical Press and Vintage for permission to reproduce extracts from publications in copyright.

Finally, my special thanks go to my wife Margaret for her support and encouragement with the book.

INTRODUCTION

Most readers of this book will be engaged in commissioning or purchasing care in one way or another. That could be as a social worker, a team leader or a commissioning manager. It is a tough task and finding time to read anything is quite an achievement, especially when it is hardly reading for relaxation if one picks up a book about work.

It always seems a bit presumptuous for an author to offer advice on how to use the book. Surely it is enough that the book is being read without having to proffer detailed instructions as well. My excuse is that the suggestions on how best to use the book are designed to save time for the reader and make life easier.

The first chapter sets the scene. Those familiar with the story of the last fifteen years may choose to skip it. I believe, however, that history has lessons for us even if every generation chooses to make its own set of mistakes. The language of commissioning and its influence can be traced back to the Griffiths Report. It is important to mark just how great have been the shifts in attitude and in responsibilities of social services departments. Far from being dinosaurs resistant to change, they have shown a remarkable capacity for change and continuous development which reflects well on their political and professional leadership.

The final chapter is an attempt to map the changes and challenges which face social care in the next few years which will affect both the content and the organizational context of commissioning.

In between is the meat of the book with chapters designed to help the commissioner make sense of the different aspects of their role. Each chapter contains case studies and activities. Providing examples to illustrate what can be done can help to illuminate. The case studies aim to provide illustrative material to back up what is contained in the text. They are an amalgam drawn from material in several different agencies. They do not describe any single local authority. Sometimes the course of action is clear from the text but where it is not I have set out the key ideas in Chapter 9.

The activities or exercises are designed for possible use in a classroom or seminar setting. They can be undertaken as written tasks, or they can be used as the basis for discussion. In Chapter 9 I have provided a checklist of key points which could have been taken into account. They are not fully comprehensive answers and you may well have thought of other relevant points. Commissioning does not lend itself to scores out of ten. My answers are suggestions to think about.

And thinking is what this book is about. The pressure to act in social care is so powerful because the circumstances of the service users are often so desperate that thinking time is at a premium. Yet if the book is to be distilled into one simple message, it is that commissioning well is about thinking well, exploring options and balancing a variety of interests. If you stop to think before acting in your commissioning role, this book will be worthwhile.

CHAPTER 1

PUTTING PURCHASING IN CONTEXT

OBJECTIVES

By the end of this chapter you should be able to:

▪ Understand how the concept of the enabling role of social services developed.

▪ Appreciate the significance of the Griffiths Report (1988) and the 1990 NHS and Community Care Act in shaping the new direction for social services departments.

▪ Know the distinction between commissioning and purchasing.

▪ Be able to identify some of the core skills needed to discharge a purchasing role.

THE ROLE OF SOCIAL SERVICES DEPARTMENTS

When social services departments were established following the Local Authority Social Services Act 1970, few thought about the departments as purchasers except in the sense of the traditional function of purchasing paper clips, stationery and filing cabinets. Only in the last decade have the scale and significance of the purchasing function been fully recognized. The result is that many staff working in local authorities have little specific training and limited understanding of this aspect of the role.

The initial task of social services departments was to draw together a variety of disparate functions which had been carried out by the children's department, the welfare department and mental welfare services to meet the needs of different client groups. As articulated in the Seebohm Report (1968) which preceded the legislation, the aim of the department was to do the following:

(a)   Meet needs on the basis of the total requirements of the individual or family rather than on the basis of a limited set of symptoms.
(b)   Provide a clear and comprehensive pattern of responsibility over the whole field.
(c)   Attract more resources.
(d)   Use those resources more effectively.
(e)   Generate adequate recruitment and training of the staff skills which are, or may become, necessary.
(f)   Meet needs at present being neglected.
(g)   Adapt to changing conditions.
(h)   Provide a better organisation for collecting and disseminating information relevant to the development of the social services.
(i)   Be more accessible and comprehensible to those who need to use them.

(Seebohm 1968: 219)

That list of tasks remains relevant over thirty years later. Despite the barrage of criticism which has fallen on social services departments following child abuse scandals, many of the objectives set in the Seebohm Report have been achieved. The entire report, however, was focused on the organization and delivery of services within the public sector and was silent about the independent sector with the exception of one paragraph about the role of voluntary organizations. The broader responsibility of departments to respond to social need by orchestrating a range of resources had yet to be developed.

THE GROWTH OF THE PRIVATE SECTOR

Social policy often evolves in an unplanned way. The scale of child abuse and in particular child sexual abuse was unrecognized when departments were established. The role of residential homes in providing care for a range of client groups was unquestioned. The implicit assumption was that the great majority of care would be provided in the public sector which could offer security and safeguards for vulnerable people. Change came not though explicit public policy, but through a social security loophole.

In the early 1980s each local social security office had a local limit for all forms of board and lodging with a discretionary power to meet the full cost. As offices made wider use of that discretion new limits were set in 1983 for residential care and nursing homes with the limit set at 'the highest reasonable charge' for suitable accommodation in the area. This led to a rapid escalation in cost as few social security officials were able or willing to reject charges as unreasonable. No assessment was made of whether the residents in homes needed that form of care. Further changes were made in 1985 with an attempt to limit the soaring expenditure by setting nationally determined limits according to the type of residential home. Homes for people with a physical disability had a higher limit than those for learning disability, which in turn were higher than for substance misuse with mental health next in the hierarchy of charges. The lowest limit set for homes was for those for the care of the elderly. Nursing homes rates were set at a higher level.

The attempt to control expenditure by setting national limits came too late. The genie was out of the bottle. The numbers of residents in private and voluntary homes funded in this way grew sixfold in six years between 1978 and 1984, and the annual cost to the Exchequer rose from £6 million to £200 million (Audit Commission 1986: 115) in the same period. Local authority and voluntary sector bed numbers remained unchanged while private sector places more than doubled.

For private proprietors Christmas came early year after year. They were able to admit all those who wished to go into residential care. They could do so knowing that the State would pick up the bill for those below the capital threshold. At the same time the underlying capital value of the residential home was itself rising rapidly in an inflationary property market.

The effect was to create a series of what the Audit Commission described as perverse incentives. State support was available for residential care but not available to support people in their own homes. People were admitted to residential care who did not require the intensive help available there. The higher funding level of nursing care encouraged growth in that area. In its trenchant analysis the Audit Commission argued that it would not be tenable to do nothing about the financial organizational and staffing arrangements for community care. It was, however, to be seven years after the Audit Commission report before a new system was put in place!

Sir Roy Griffiths was asked by the government to undertake a review of the organization of community care. His recommendation that 'major restructuring can be disruptive and time-consuming' (Griffiths Report 1988: iv) and that structural change should be rejected as premature and over-prescriptive led to a recommendation that social services departments should have the primary role in designing purchasing and organizing community care. This role should be financed through a special government grant to be financed from social security expenditure.

His report waited a long time for a government response. It was not to the taste of Ministers. First, it located responsibility with local government, an institution heartily disliked by the Prime Minister Mrs Thatcher. Second, it imposed controls on the private sector by setting criteria for admission to residential care. Third, it represented a transfer of spending from central to local government. A fierce Whitehall battle took place before legislative proposals were brought forward in the NHS and Community Care Act 1990.

Even then, further delay ensued as the Chancellor delayed implementation for a year to allow more time for preparation as nervousness remained about local government capacity to do the job. Six months prior to implementation Virginia Bottomley, the Secretary of State for Health, announced that the transferred resources in the shape of a Special Transitional Grant would be ring fenced and could not be spent on education, highways or other aspects of local government services. This was to meet the anxiety that local government would use the additional resources to fund a spending expansion in other areas.

THE ENABLING ROLE

The battle for control tended to obscure aspects of the Griffiths Report which were arguably of greater long-term significance. For the first time Griffiths set the enabling role of social services at the heart of its function. The concept of enabling had been trailed earlier by Norman Fowler, when Secretary of State for Health.

Ministerial speeches to social services conferences are usually a bland recitation of new policy initiatives. They rarely require much thought by the audience. At the Buxton conference of the Association of Directors of Social Services in 1984, Norman Fowler broke the mould. In a wide-ranging speech he called for a different model of care. He argued that social services should switch their focus from that of the direct provision of care to one of funding and facilitating the delivery of care.

Fowler suggested that there were three paramount responsibilities for social services departments:

1   A comprehensive strategic view of all available sources of care.
2   A recognition that direct services were only part of the local pattern.
3   A recognition that social services should support and promote the fullest possible participation of the other different sources of care that exist or which can be called into being.

(Fowler 1984)

What the Griffiths Report proposed was, however, a more fully worked-out model which drew on American experience. The USA has a long-standing tradition of welfare pluralism. The not-for-profit sector provides services often with a religious or ethnic affiliation. The profit sector is also more developed offering services to individuals for fee or to public sector organizations under contract. Herbert Laming, later to be Chief Inspector of Social Services in the Department of Health, was an adviser to Sir Roy Griffiths. Shortly before the report was commissioned he had undertaken a study tour to the USA to examine service contracting. That experience is reflected in the report's proposals.

Griffiths was explicit. He asserted a desire that his proposals should 'encourage a proportionate increase in private and voluntary services as distinct from directly provided services' (Griffiths Report 1988: 7). The gains which he saw as flowing from this shift were: choice, flexibility, innovation and competition. In other words, the creation of a market, however imperfect, in social care would produce benefits for service users. Sir Roy's background in supermarkets led some critics to argue that the users of social services could not be regarded as consumers in the same way as shoppers. The degree to which users can be given genuine choice is still debated. But the key concept articulated by Griffiths has underpinned the development of purchasing and contracting in the new world of community care.

The template for the future pattern of services was set by the White Paper, *Caring for People* (Department of Health 1989). This proposed the idea of care packages drawn up to meet the needs of individuals and supporting independent living in their own homes. This flexibility was contrasted with the service-led approach in which a basket of services was available which were organized and delivered to meet the convenience of providers rather than users. The packages should 'make use wherever possible of services from the voluntary, not for profit and private providers insofar as this represents cost-effective care choice' (ibid.: 22). The role of social services departments was to stimulate and encourage diversity of provision particularly in the non-residential sector. The diversity had already been achieved in the residential sector by the rapid expansion of provision.

The financial mechanism adopted for the transfer of resources from the social security budget to local government was the subject of much debate, both in relation to the calculation of the transfer sum and the nature of its payment. Eventually the government announced that the transferred resources would take place over a five-year period with a grant payable to local authorities calculated on a formula based on current usage of residential care, the population of vulnerable care groups and a variety of other factors (the group working out proposals for the formula was unsurprisingly named 'the algebra group'). For local government which had been looking forward to the transferred resources as a means of developing new services the sting came in the tail in the form of the conditions attached to the Special Transitional Grant: 85 per cent of the grant had to be spent in the independent sector.

This seemed to be something less than a level playing field. Independent sector providers already benefited from a residential care allowance of £50 per week, and were now clearly designated as providers of choice for the transferred resources. Despite the protests of the local authority associations, the government held to its line. The net result has been a further shift in the overall balance of expenditure between directly provided services and those in the independent sector. The retreat from direct service provision in the residential sector has gathered pace with transfers of existing homes to housing associations and voluntary care providers, and occasionally to the private sector.

The scale of the shift which followed the Griffiths Report has been dramatic. The proportion of all residential care beds provided by the public sector fell in England from 44 per cent in 1988 to 18 per cent in 1998. Similar trends are evident in Wales and Scotland where a higher baseline of local authority provision was evident. For example, Wales has seen a drop from 51 per cent to 33 per cent between 1988 and 1998, and Scotland a drop from 57 per cent to 35 per cent. The private sector now provides over 60 per cent of available beds.

As discussed above, Griffiths saw choice as a major advantage of a more plural welfare system. The user's right to choice in relation to residential care was enshrined in a statutory direction giving users the right to have their choice of home. The choice was not unfettered. It was the exercise of choice within the financial parameters set by the authority.

The example below gives an illustration of how choice may not always be real.

CASE STUDY 1: CHOICE

Mrs Smith is 93. She had a fall and fractured her femur and has since lost confidence in being able to manage the stairs at home. She lives with her widowed daughter, Mary who is 71. Mary has visited every day as the hospital is a cottage hospital less than a mile away. The GP suggests to Mary that her mother will have to go into a home and Mary starts to look for a suitable place. There are three homes in the small town – one charges £100 per week more than the level set by the local authority as its maximum payment, one £30 more and one only is available within the rate. Mary visits this home and is appalled by the lack of amenities, the careworn appearance of the home and the use of TV as a 'sedative' for the residents. The home charging

£30 per week extra is better but they only have a shared room available and do not know when a vacancy will occur. Mary is worried that she will not be able to afford the extra out of her small occupational pension. When Mary discusses this with the doctor, she is encouraged to look further afield for homes.

The interplay of finance and geography means that the statutory direction on choice may be technically upheld but it does not feel like a real choice to Mary. The choice she faces is between placing her mother in an unsatisfactory home or placing her mother miles away from her few friends and from Mary herself.

The shift in the balance of care for domiciliary services was slower at first. There are several reasons for this. First, the residential care allowance was not mirrored in domiciliary care removing a crucial financial incentive for providers. Second, the returns from domiciliary care are lower because there is no capital appreciation built into the business. Third, low margins and the high turnover of staff, usually among the lowest paid in social care, make it difficult to sustain quality care and programmes for training and development. Fourth, the nature of the domiciliary care market is very different. The emergence of the private sector in domiciliary care has been more patchy geographically than in the residential sector.

In Central London the private market is underdeveloped; in some rural areas there are a number of localized providers specific to the county. There are few equivalents to the major providers of long-term care in the private sector operating on a national basis. But despite the slow initial progress, the cumulative impact of the shift from public provision has been equally dramatic. A study by Laing and Buisson in 2000 noted: 'eight years ago before the reforms, social services delivered 98% of the home care they funded. Now it is down to 49%' (*Community Care*, 2–8 November 2000).

THE DRIVE TO EXTERNALIZE SERVICES

The drive to externalize services to the private sector was seen by successive Secretaries of State of both parties as offering better services for the same or reduced costs. In one sense this is surprising as the application of privatization approaches to welfare provision has been deeply unpopular. A rational debate about the appropriate role of the private sector in care has been impaired by the ideological gulf between protagonists. What is clear is that this touches a sensitive nerve in public consciousness. Gilbert (1983) suggests that the distaste for the private sector is, first, because pecuniary motives are influencing the care normally given by families from loyalty, love and affection and, second, because there is a deep suspicion that the needs and welfare of the individual will be subordinated to financial considerations.

This ideological polarization is an important issue for purchasers because sugges- tions made in the best interests of the client can be ascribed to other motives if they involve the private sector. In working with clients and their relatives where the private sector is involved as a partner, it will often be necessary to give extra reassurance about the quality of care and the safeguards available in the event of failure to perform as expected.

The advent of a new government in 1997 with a strong historic commitment to the public sector was widely welcomed in local government circles. Some local government polls suggested that 90 per cent of local government officers had voted against the Conservative Government. This followed not only years of severe financial restrictions but also years of denigration from Prime Minister Mrs Thatcher and her local government ministers. The commitment to abolish compulsory competitive tendering (CCT) by Labour was seen as a declaration of goodwill to local government interests. Things have not turned out quite as planned.

The device selected by the Labour Government as an alternative to CCT was Best Value. This way of improving standards and driving down costs has been developed as founded on four Cs – challenge, compare, consult and compete. The challenge was to establish whether the service was needed and why. The comparison was a cost and quality comparison with similar services provided by other authorities. Consultation with the public and service users was a key element in testing the validity of conclusions.

The fourth C – competition – was seen as a residual sanction in the event of default but is emerging as a more potent threat to the independence of local government than had been imagined. The blame and shame model of inspection and scrutiny epitomized by OFSTED was regarded as a success and its former head, Chris Woodhead, was highly regarded for his adherence to high standards and the vigour with which he denounced failing schools and failing teachers. Schools and education authorities which fail will be stripped of their responsibility for provision. The clear implication in both health and social services is that similar treatment will be meted out to those seen as failing to deliver the modernization agenda. The rhetoric with its implicit assumption that the private sector is more efficient and more cost-effective than the public sector is scarcely distinguishable from that of its predecessors.

What is it about the public sector which so frustrates governments of all political complexions? And why are social services such a particular source of frustration? The first and in some ways most important explanation is that these services are not directly subject to government control. Unlike the National Health Service, personal social services are a major local government function. Subject to meeting statutory duties, local authorities have discretion both over the type of services they provide and their level. The clear subtext of the National Health Service Plan published in July 2000 is that such variations are no longer acceptable.

Local authority discretion has produced what in the context of the NHS has been described as the postcode lottery – wide variations in the thresholds of social service intervention, in the volume of provision, in the eligibility criteria for service and in attitudes to the independent sector.

The modernization agenda in social services aims to achieve higher standards and greater consistency across the country. The National Care Standards Commission is designed to ensure greater consistency in relation to registration and inspection of the independent sector, The Performance Assessment Framework sets national performance indicators for social services authorities. The General Social Care Council will produce codes of conduct for employers and staff. And Best Value will provide a tool with which to secure improvement in poorly performing authorities. As Best Value will itself be subject to external inspection, the room for independent action on the part of local authorities is becoming more circumscribed. Social services departments are increasingly seen by government as delivering a national service which is locally administered.

The second reason for discontent with public sector performance is the slowness of change. This is most evident in the area of adoption. Again, the Blair Government is following the mantra of its predecessor in the belief that local authority political correctness is standing in the way of large numbers of children in care who could be adopted. This is based on the tabloid stories about mixed race couples rejected because of their lack of race awareness, and potential adoptive parents rejected because of smoking, their age or being overweight, allegedly because of the views of politically correct social workers. Such stories are matched by stories of gay couples being approved as adopters. In practice, social workers have continued to seek the best solution for each child but this has neither brought an end to tabloid criticism nor an increase in the numbers of children adopted.

This failure to translate a policy objective into results is for the third reason that governments struggle with the public sector. The business of change is more complex than is readily understood by political leaders. Translating the government's broad vision into policy and then into action requires a deliberate and measured attempt to build consensus, and to win practitioners to support the changes in practice required. A litany of exhortation, threats and sanctions is unlikely to be effective in bringing about long-term attitudinal shifts.

This analysis is important because it sets out the background to a policy framework in which the private sector is likely to play an increasing role, both as a sanction through enforced competition against failing authorities and as the preferred vehicle for new initiatives. Youth justice services have been hived off to a new agency, the Youth Justice Board. Adoption is another area where the failure to deliver on governmental objectives has led to exploration of removing the function from local authorities and giving it to a private sector-led agency. For the time being the government has decided to rely on procedural change and new targets as its method of achieving change.

ACTIVITY 1.1: FACTORS DRIVING CHANGE

The share of personal social services delivered through the independent sector has steadily increased over the past twenty years.

1 Identify the factors which have contributed to this trend and list them in order of importance.
2 Based on the material you have read, what is the likely trend over the next twenty years and what are the factors driving change?

ORGANIZING SOCIAL SERVICES

The development of the enabling role meant that local authority social services departments were enjoined to take a strategic view in planning service development. This was not their first experience of strategic planning. Twenty-five years earlier they had been asked to draw up ten-year plans predicated on the assumption of a 10 per cent per annum growth – a rate of expansion far in advance of that given to the NHS in recent

Budgets. The collapse of that planning assumption in the wake of the oil crisis of 1974 led many authorities to be chary of written commitments on which they would be unable to deliver. The NHS and Community Care Act 1990 required authorities to prepare a Community Care plan for submission to the Department of Health. Detailed guidance was given on the preparation of the plans which were to be prepared in conjunction with health authorities and were to cover common objectives for particular care groups, funding agreements, agreed policy on key operational areas and a framework for development. While the emphasis was on collaborative work with health, subsequent guidance called for greater emphasis on the needs of carers, the involvement of the independent sector and evidence of the involvement of user interests.

In its initial guidance the Department of Health called for a 'clear distinction to be made between purchasing and providing roles' (Department of Health 1989: 23). A similar division had been introduced in the NHS through the creation of self-governing trusts with the District Health Authority having a strategic and funding role but with service delivery the responsibility of the trusts. While the Department stopped short of calling for a new local authority service for service delivery, it encouraged organizational changes to offer a clear separation between purchasing and providing roles. The power of the proposed split was the belief that services were too wedded to provider interests and unresponsive to the needs of users and carers. This is a recurrent theme in central government thinking about local government.

Not all local authorities followed the departmental guidance but a number did effect a formal split between purchasing and providing. The absence of any visible improvements as a result of the split in driving forward the development of the independent sector meant that a rigid separation of roles has become less fashionable over time. Instead the purchasing function has been subsumed into a broader commissioning role.

COMMISSIONING

The Department of Health definition of commissioning was 'a strategic activity of assessing needs, resources and current services and developing a strategy of how to make best use of available resources to meet needs' (Department of Health: 1995a). Commissioning is a broader activity than that of purchasing which is only one aspect of the commissioning task, which is sometimes but not always delegated to specialist staff, at least where a formal contract is involved. The two activities are, however, closely intertwined as purchasing from the independent sector has to be a part of a coherent commissioning strategy.

In 1995 a Department of Health circular booklet and guidance were published (Department of Health 1995a, 1995b). These offered some help in disentangling the various roles involved in the commissioning process. Table 1.1 develops that guidance.

Since 1995 a marked emphasis has been placed on the development of joint commissioning with health. Frank Dobson as Secretary of State frequently denounced the Berlin Wall which he saw between health and social services, contributing to the problem of delayed discharge from hospital for elderly patients. In reality, the direction on choice, however imperfect, was more frequently the problem as elderly people waited for a place in a home of their choice rather than one chosen for them by social services.

Table 1.1 Roles in the commissioning process

Role	Definition
Commissioning	A strategic view of services and resources set against needs, and a plan to get the best fit from available resources
Collaborative commissioning	Commissioning in which two or more authorities work together to pursue shared objectives, and deploy resources in concert to achieve those objectives
Joint commissioning	Commissioning involving two or more authorities sharing objectives and resources as in a pooled budget
Purchasing	The process of acquiring goods or services at an agreed price, defined quality and to a specific timescale
Contracting	The formal legally binding agreement between purchaser and provider of services, which needs to incorporate the service specifications defined in the purchasing process
Providing	The provision of services which may be by public, private or voluntary sector agencies. It will be subject to a form of agreement which may take the form of legally binding contracts, service agreements or grant conditions dependent on the nature and scale of service provided

The frustration caused by the boundary disputes came to a head in the continuing care agreements. Although discharge arrangements had not been a central preoccupation in the wake of the immediate introduction of community care, they were emphasized in the joint letters from the Chief Executive of the NHS and the Chief Inspector of Social Services. These annual letters set out a number of key tasks for both health and local authorities, presaging the joint priorities set by the Labour Government in 1998 and subsequent years. The requirement to draw up a continuing care agreement was designed to clarify respective roles and responsibilities, and set out an agreed threshold for residential and nursing care.

This apparently simple exercise caused acute difficulties in many areas. Not only were there tensions over definitions and demarcations but also over the level of resources. The level of resources available to social services is more susceptible to volatility than that of resources available to health. First, the annual local government settlement has until recently been subject to annual changes of formula with sometimes marked variations in patterns of distribution favouring types of authority. Second, the legacy of capping has limited the power of local authorities to raise revenue through the council tax. Third, the annual increase for local government resources has been less year on year than that made available for health. Fourth, local political factors will influence patterns of allocation between services. As a result, social services are less able to enter into long-term commitments. The close monitoring by the Department of Health eventually ensured the completion of the process of continuing care agreements but it served as a further reinforcement of the gap between the two services.

The degree to which delayed discharges have become a fault line between the two services with primary responsibility ascribed to the failings of social services can be seen in the NHS Plan where ministers make it clear that they will no longer accept boundary disputes between the services as an alibi for inaction.

The incoming government initially had taken a different tack in pursuing the collaborative objective. It introduced joint priorities for the two services; it introduced bi-annual monitoring by the Department of Health Regional Office and the Social Services Inspectorate; it introduced performance assessment frameworks for both services; and it brought forward the Health Act 1999 which offered new possibilities for collaboration through pooled budgets, integrated commissioning and joint provision. These sensible initiatives had previously been blocked by inflexibilities built into NHS legislation.

The NHS Plan in 2000 took a tougher line. The voluntary partnership agreements based on the new flexibilities were introduced in April 2000. By July in the same year they were deemed to be failing to secure the pace of change required and were made mandatory. New Care Trusts were proposed to draw together health and social services with a clear statement that the imposition of these trusts would be used as a sanction against those authorities making little progress towards partnership. The Minister of State John Hutton said that he expected that all social care would be delivered through Care Trusts within five years (Neate 2000).

THE GROWTH OF THE CONTRACT CULTURE

The phrase 'the contract culture' has been widely used to describe the shift which followed the 1990 NHS and Community Care Act to more extensive use of private and voluntary sector providers. We have seen that the growth in the 1980s was predominantly in the private sector, but the framework envisaged in the legislation had huge implications for the voluntary sector. With the exception of residential care providers in the voluntary sector, the great majority of voluntary organizations had offered services which were funded by a combination of annual support from grants and local fund-raising activities. Such locally based voluntary bodies had been seen as part of the network of active citizenship underpinning statutory services. These groups saw the community care legislation as a threat implying loss of control, direct accountability to social services and a consequent compromising of their independence. This was further compounded by what was viewed by some commentators as a retreat by the State from its responsibility for direct provision with a consequent expectation that the independent sector would become the provider by default.

More welcome was the emphasis placed on the creation of new not-for-profit providers. The requirement that 85 per cent of the Special Transitional Grant had to be spent in the independent sector meant that a number of creative ways were explored of meeting the requirement without losing significant local authority influence on the provision of services. These included management buy-outs and cooperatives. The two most significant new models of provision have been the development of arm's-length trusts to manage residential care and the development of care services by housing associations. While some housing associations have developed extensive domiciliary care services, the overall pattern of provision has changed less than had been anticipated. The initial enthusiasm of the more entrepreneurial mangers in the independent sector has also been muted as the full implications of the contract culture became apparent.

Instead of the diversity and choice which Griffith had hoped to promote through the expansion of the independent sector, the smaller providers have tended to be gobbled up by the larger. This is true both in residential and domiciliary care where major economies of scale in management can be achieved if a critical mass of provision is secured. The consolidation of major care providers responsible for thousands of beds has thus been mirrored by a growing number of small local providers withdrawing from the market because of the increasing burden of registration requirements on their costs. Local authorities have maintained downward pressure on costs driven by their difficult financial situation. In this context even the publicly quoted care providers have struggled to sustain profitability.

Why has a truly competitive market been slow to develop? First, it was not always politically popular. Some local authorities circumvented the requirements of the Special Transitional Grant by hiving off their homes into a not-for-profit trust operating at arm's length from the local authority. They saw this option which gave them substantial influence over the company as preferable to wholesale reliance on the market. Second, the market is volatile because of its vulnerability to shifts in the availability of public support. This can come because of national or local financial restrictions. Third, the providers do not have direct relationships with councils or councillors but with purchasers who may have their own idiosyncrasies. They also have to negotiate a relationship with the local Registration and Inspection unit. This has been a source of sustained criticism from the independent sector about wide variations in approach. The advent of a Care Standards Commission setting national standards should ameliorate some of these problems.

In a review of social services Douglas and Philpot pose a question about the impact of the market on choice:

> Will access to services diminish and greater choice prove an illusion as larger providers, less interested in innovation and more attuned to the need to maximise income, push smaller ones to the margins and even out of business?
>
> (1998: 200)

The evidence is that this is happening and the number of owner-managed providers is contracting in both residential and domiciliary care.

Just as the Griffiths Report drew heavily upon American experience, so too the voluntary sector has expressed its concern about the potential impact of the mixed economy based on visits to the USA. Gutch (1992) noted that larger organizations tended to benefit from a more competitive environment because they possessed skills in writing proposals and delivering realistic targets. In contrast, smaller groups were tending to be squeezed out. He also expressed anxiety that the contracting process itself was focused on the delivery of a service rather than on monitoring the outcome for service users. The advent of competition had served to drive down costs rather than to encourage diversity of provision.

Harding and Phillips suggested that the most successful examples of the market working effectively for older people in the USA offered:

> A firm system of local planning, based on a shared value base, which has controlled regulated and developed local services. The areas where such

local planning exists can demonstrate greater consumer satisfaction, greater equity of access and better cost control and value for money.

(1996: 40)

Looking at the fears which have been expressed is helpful in providing clues to successful purchasing. While partnership is a much over-used word, it accurately describes the mutuality of interest between purchasers and providers in securing effective services. The confrontational approach to contracting which some purchasers adopted based on the model in use for building contracts, which invariably seem to end in claims and counter-claims, has no relevance for social care. Unfortunately too many of those in purchasing roles tended to take a macho approach to their role. The list below will be developed in more detail in subsequent chapters but is a summary of what makes for successful purchasing:

- *Shared values*: the purchase of social care is not a commercial transaction. The purchaser rarely has the range of choice of a supermarket shopper able to make a judgement between price and quality. But what they do have is a shared value base in which the interest of the service user and the quality of service which they receive are the paramount considerations. That value base in turn can be reflected both in the service specification and contract and in the style of engagement between purchaser and provider.

- *Knowledge of the market*: purchasers need to understand the current range of services, the strategy for future development and to understand what type of service is required to deliver that strategy. They need to understand the mix between public sector and independent sector provision, and the range of providers involved in the independent sector. They also need to know the strengths and weaknesses of current providers.

- *Understanding costs*: the cost of services is more than the unit cost charged to purchasers. The advantage to local authorities of retaining some in-house provision is that this makes it possible to understand clearly the cost base of the private sector. There are as many dangers for those responsible for commissioning services in unrealistic pricing by providers as in padded pricing structures. The opportunity cost to the local authority of a contract failing or having to be terminated is high.

- *Fairness*: this sounds axiomatic. Purchasers are subject to local authority rules but these tend to govern the formal stage when a tender is submitted. Even more important is fairness at the preliminary stage. A standard set of information should be available to all interested in providing services. Even where a well-known current provider or an in-house tenderer is involved, the purchaser must be careful to ensure that nobody has an inside track with information given to one provider that is not available to all. Great care is necessary both to be equitable and to be seen to be equitable.

- *Openness*: after the strictures about fairness one might conclude that a safety-first approach would dictate minimal communication. Not so, for the first suggestion offered was partnership. Partnerships are built on the basis of trust. The aim in purchasing care is to get the best available service at a price the authority is able and willing to pay. That is best secured through being as open as possible about the constraints, difficulties and objectives of the purchased service. As long as the approach is even-handed, there is much to gain from giving as much background information to the provider as possible.

The qualities outlined have to be buttressed by a range of technical skills in service specification, contract writing, pricing and outcome monitoring but constitute the essential basis for effective purchasing.

ACTIVITY 1.2: WORKING WITH PROVIDERS

Apply the qualities set out above to this scenario. You have been asked to develop a flexible care at home service particularly covering weekends and evenings. This is part of the authority's domiciliary care strategy. An initial request for expressions of interest has brought three responses from:

1 a local voluntary organization which runs clubs for the elderly, houses a carers support group and a day service for children with disabilities
2 a group of home care workers and their manager interested in running the service themselves but not constituted as a company
3 a subsidiary care organization of a major provider of private residential care homes. The subsidiary has been newly formed and has no track record in care at home.

How would you approach the discussions with potential providers? Map each provider against the five principles set out above. Where would you anticipate difficulties? How far would it be proper to go in supporting the in-house team with legal and financial advice to enable them to mount an effective bid?

KEY POINTS

☐ The purchasing role is both one of the most complex but also one of the most politically sensitive tasks within a local authority.

☐ The mixed economy of welfare provision has developed rapidly in the past fifteen years.

☐ This shift will continue because of the continuing pressure to reduce costs.

☐ Purchasing is one part of commissioning.

☐ Key attributes of successful purchasing are knowledge of the market, understanding costs, skills in negotiation and a sense of fairness.

☐ Purchasing tasks fit with the broader field of commissioning because purchasing is the way in which commissioning strategy is translated into practical action.

KEY READING

The report by Sir Roy Griffiths, *Community Care: Agenda for Action* (1988) is a model of clarity, crispness and common sense. A general introduction to the work of social care can be found in *Caring and Coping* (1998) by Douglas and Philpot which has many useful case examples to illustrate its argument. Hill's *Local Authority Social Services: An Introduction* (2000) is a useful source text with a particularly helpful piece by Stephen Mitchell analysing the modernization agenda. The shift to the mixed economy and its implications are best captured in *Social Care in a Mixed Economy* (1994) by Wistow and colleagues. *Community Care* (1998) by Means and Smith reflects the likely impact of the new Labour Government in its second edition. This puts the change in a broader context as do Lewis and Glennerster in *Implementing the New Community Care* (1996).

CHAPTER 2

COMMISSIONING

OBJECTIVES

By the end of this chapter you should be able to understand:

- What commissioning involves for care managers, for strategic commissioners, and for joint commissioners.

- How to put together the key elements in a commissioning plan.

- The skills needed for commissioning.

- The different types of commissioning structures.

MICRO-COMMISSIONING

Before one gets into discussions with providers about what and how they can provide services and the niceties of contracting, purchasers need to know what they want and why. The commissioning function has to precede purchasing. The task of commissioning is to decide the future strategy and direction of services, and to identify the types of service which may be needed in future. It also involves making certain that the right mix of services is achieved with the resources available.

In the early experiments with care management before the community care reforms, the care manager had access to a team of staff bringing together care skills and home help skills to support vulnerable people at home. The idea of the multi-skilled support worker retains great appeal and the concept of integrated care teams discussed below may bring it closer to reality. Hitherto, however, the idea has rarely been successfully translated into joint working at operational level. In consequence, the care manager has more often operated as a broker putting together care from a variety of different sources.

CASE STUDY 2: FEEDING MRS BROWN

Mrs Brown lives alone in a country village. The village has a grocery store, three pubs, and a few shops selling specialist items. There is an hourly bus service to the town 8 miles away where the care manager is based. Mrs B lives in a bungalow but suffers from severe arthritis making it impossible for her to cook and clean. The home care worker visits daily. What are the options for the care manager to ensure Mrs B gets at least one hot meal a day?

Before the community care reforms, Mrs B would have been offered meals on wheels possibly five days a week, but more likely on fewer days a week. The care manager today should have a wider range of options. The meals on wheels service should now be available on a seven days a week basis but there are other options:

- The home care worker could be asked to prepare a meal and heat it so it can be taken out of the oven before the home care worker leaves.
- One of the local pubs could be approached to see if they would prepare a meal and deliver it to Mrs B possibly using a volunteer driver to pick up the meal and run it round to Mrs B. Alternatively, neighbours could be asked to prepare a meal on a regular basis for payment.
- A mix and match package could be arranged with meals on wheels two days a week, home care two days, neighbours two days and the local pub one day a week. While more complex, this does provide both variety and scope for substitution if key figures are off sick or away on holiday. It also gives the care manager a chance more clearly to understand Mrs B's own preferences.

This type of work is just as much commissioning as the task carried out by those who write strategic plans. It is known as micro-commissioning. It describes the process of developing a care package to meet the needs of the user. It is individualized and sensitive to the preferences of the user. This type of commissioning is very much that envisaged in the community care changes. It does, however, suffer from drawbacks. The first is time and the second cost.

Liaising with a number of different providers and getting costings from them is time-consuming in itself. Add to that the potential for daily amendments to the care plan through the normal vicissitudes of daily life – sickness, cars breaking down, etc. – and the time pressures on the care manager begin to multiply.

While in this instance meals provided by a neighbour are likely to be considerably cheaper than meals provided by meals on wheels, there are often economies of scale which make individually crafted services more costly. For example, where single items are being acquired from a supplier more accustomed to block contracts, the unit price will be significantly higher.

The care manager has to balance needs and resources using skills in assessment, consultation and commissioning. The task requires local knowledge and understanding of what is available through voluntary organizations as well as publicly provided services. It may involve work with local health agencies to ensure that a comprehensive care plan captures the involvement of all agencies with the service user. The care manager also needs to be alert to trends and patterns of need in the area. It may be possible to devise a response which would meet common difficulties.

SOCIAL CARE PLANNING

Commissioning happens at all levels of the organization. The team leader drawing on the knowledge of team members has a crucial role in identifying common needs in a locality to develop social care planning. Again, an example may help to clarify this aspect.

CASE STUDY 3: MEETING LOCAL NEEDS

A social services team is based in a tower block in an inner city estate. The estate has high levels of crime – mostly petty – a growing drug problem and few youth facilities. There is a high proportion of lone parent households. The local GP practice is concerned at the levels of depression on the estate. Social services caseloads reflect the problems. The team decides to press the local youth service to provide an after-school homework club as few of the children on the estate have a quiet place to do their homework. By sustained pressure they are able to put together a small project involving the school, the youth service, social services and the use of voluntary helpers to supervise the club from 3.30p.m. to 6p.m.

In the purist sense of the word this was not commissioning because it did not go through the stages of service specification, competition and contracting. Yet commissioning is not just that formal process – it is about identifying gaps and putting services and resources together to meet those gaps.

The skills required for commissioning were set out by Professor Roger Hadley in the Barclay Report (1982) when he described what was then termed social care planning:

- The ability to locate and be accessible to local networks. This requires a pooling of knowledge about the strengths of the neighbourhood, and the development of good lines of communication.
- Responsiveness and flexibility. To strengthen informal care networks, services have to be sensitive and adaptable, responding to the need presented rather than offering services on a take it or leave it basis.
- The ability to draw in additional resources by wider involvement of informal helpers, volunteers and the voluntary sector.
- Understanding and working with people and groups.

These qualities and characteristics have been consistently recycled since the Barclay Report. The new emphasis on users and carers, the importance of community consultation in developing Best Value and the wider use of the independent sector which has underpinned the development of community care policies can all be traced back to the concepts articulated by Hadley.

STRATEGIC COMMISSIONING

At a strategic policy level the commissioning role is governed by the ever-increasing number of statutory plans required by the government. The list includes the Children's Services plan, the review of services to the under-eights, the Community Care plan, the Joint Investment Plan required for each care group, the Drug Action Team annual plan, the Youth Offending annual plan, the Community Safety annual plan, the local performance plan and the series of action plans required to satisfy the latest government initiative. All this begs the question – where does planning end and commissioning begin?

Plans are the staple diet of local government. They describe the desired objective, relate it to local and national strategies, and set out a timescale and milestones for the achievement of the plan. Commissioning is the process whereby plans are translated into action. It involves decisions about the mix and pattern of services to achieve the policy objective; it involves decisions about the balance of services and the use of the mixed economy of welfare provision to achieve the objectives; it involves securing quality standards in provision and monitoring performance; and it may involve the initiation of authority-wide moves to bring in new providers whether by a tendering exercise or some other way.

CASE STUDY 4: DEVELOPING A COMMISSIONING PLAN

Midshire is a predominantly rural county with five population centres with around 100,000 people in each. The total population is 800,000. After a long period of one party control the council is now hung. The Joint Review team visited last year and were very critical of the dependence on in-house services for all client groups and how little had been done to encourage a mixed economy in provision. Cuts in Standard Spending Assessment mean that the county has to make overall savings of about 3 per cent per annum for the next four years. The great majority of residential homes provided by the county fall short of registration standards and require major capital works. Some 85 per cent of domiciliary care is delivered in-house with the private sector used only at weekends and in the evenings. The county is divided into five localities to which budgets have been allocated on a historical basis. Wide discrepancies in levels of provision have resulted with, for example, one locality having double the level of residential care as another but comparable provision in home care.

How would you approach the task of drawing up a commissioning plan for services to older people? What factors would you need to take into account?

The factors which would need to be considered are:

- equity between localities
- efficiency in the use of resources
- scope for securing provision at a lower cost
- the mix of welfare provision and the robustness of the local market in care
- local political factors

Equity

The pursuit of absolute equity between localities is an impossible dream. Equity does not mean equality. Differing population mixes, different patterns of health service and independent sector provision and different distributions of wealth and income mean that no two areas have the same need for service. Equity, however, remains a valid goal for commissioners in the sense that gross disparities of provision or resources, which will often be for historical reasons, have to be addressed. The time period over which one seeks to achieve greater equity is a fine political judgement. Where there are two localities with similar characteristics but one has twice the level of resources, it would be reasonable to expect a shift of at least 3–5 per cent a year from the well off to the less well off locality over a five-year period.

Efficiency in the use of resources

One argument invariably advanced when issues of redistribution come into play is efficiency in the use of resources. By efficiency in the context of work with older people we mean:

- reaching all those in need of a service through good information and communication systems
- clear and accurate assessment processes to ensure that services reach those most in need and that there is equitable access to services
- good budgeting systems to ensure that all available resources are monitored and appropriately targeted
- clear review systems to ensure that recipients of services do not 'stay on the list' indefinitely once their needs have been met

In domiciliary care one aspect of efficiency will be the relationship between coverage – the proportion of the target population over 65 or 75 receiving a service – and intensity – the proportion of recipients receiving service of more than ten hours a week. Some areas may have large coverage but very low intensity; others may offer a very intensive service but to few recipients. There may be a Third Way between these extremes!

In residential care the unit costs of placements, the proportion of the target population in residential or nursing home settings, and the level of delayed discharges would all be looked at as part of an efficiency scrutiny.

Cost

Cost is one element in efficiency but not the only one. Ways of delivering an equivalent service at lower cost or a better service at the same cost should be constantly scrutinized. This could involve a reorganization of how tasks are undertaken to streamline the process. One way of doing this is by tackling professional or occupational demarcation lines by blurring role boundaries and thus reducing the number of people who have contact with the client. Two other fruitful areas where costs can be examined in detail are labour costs and procurement costs.

Particularly in local government the complexity of pay scales causes difficulty for commissioners. National scales are sometimes overlaid by local agreements covering such items as weekend, overtime and bank holiday working, allowances for travel and uniform costs and special responsibility payments. The true labour costs of a service will therefore be very much higher than the hourly rate of standard staff pay. A number of authorities have reduced costs both in terms of direct labour costs and administrative costs by buying out these enhancements with a one-off payment and an increase in the basic rate of pay as partial compensation. The cost of such packages means that few savings are achieved in the first year but major savings are made as new staff are hired on the revised and less costly pay scales.

Procurement costs are a major item in residential settings. There are often wide variations in the cost of provisions, heating costs and maintenance. While the commissioner will want to avoid a one-size-fits-all approach, standard unit costs have to be examined so that variations can be identified and explained. Setting a benchmark target for the higher spenders will sometimes be sufficient in itself to bring a sense of discipline into procurement practice.

The mix of welfare provision

This varies from authority to authority and locality to locality. There is no pre-set formula to provide the ideal mix. The commissioner will need to compare patterns of provision with neighbouring and with comparable authorities sharing similar socio-economic characteristics. Given the state of Midshire's homes and the capital investment required, a rapid shift in the balance of care is needed. The commissioner will want to explore with both the private for-profit sector and the not-for-profit voluntary sector the possibility of their taking over some of the existing homes or offering a block contract in their existing provision to Midshire. The creation of an arm's-length trust to manage the Midshire homes will also be explored as will the scope for extending independent sector provision of domiciliary care services. Understanding the market, how it is made up and the priorities of the key players, is essential.

Politics

This is the element which is often omitted in writings about commissioning. Politics is the art of the possible, and commissioning also is not a pure science. A commissioning plan has therefore to acknowledge the constraints on achievement. If closure of 80 per cent of the residential homes is the desired outcome in order to finance the major shift in the balance of care and the development of new services, that will be extremely unpopular with politicians. The case for change and the possible phasing of that change need to be carefully prepared.

Planning care for older people is not the exclusive responsibility of the local authority. The lead role given to local authorities in the preparation of the Community Care plan has been overtaken by the NHS lead responsibility for joint investment plans for each care group and the overarching Health Improvement Programme. The assessment of the best mix of provision will therefore need to look at any impact on delayed discharges, at the NHS provision of continuing care, at the implications for the continuing care agreement and admission criteria for residential care, and the availability of rehabilitation services and community nursing.

COMMISSIONING SKILLS

Commissioning well is a complex process requiring skills of analysis, costing, negotiation and political sensitivity.

Analysis

The core problem faced by Midshire is too much residential provision of poor physical quality, some of which is in the wrong place. That is compounded by financial pressures. The change required is therefore both a change in the pattern of care but also one which delivers real savings.

The benchmarking necessary under Best Value reviews is a good starting point. In addition to looking at the mix of provision in neighbouring or comparable counties, what level of independent provision do they have? Is it purchased under a block contract or through spot purchasing? What are the political problems in seeking greater involvement of the independent sector? Could these be eased if the provider was a voluntary body as opposed to a for-profit provider? Is an arm's-length company model feasible?

From the answers to these questions and discussions with colleagues in health, finance and social services, one can begin to develop a possible model. This will need to be based on changing the mix of care over a five-year period with clear agreed milestones for change. The timetable will be critically dependent on costings.

Costing change

Costing change is not a precise science. Few costs are certain. One of the few certainties is that change will take longer to achieve than was first thought. This is not through malevolence or ill will but almost invariably something will crop up which had not been expected in the project plan. It could be delays in securing planning consent, the discovery of asbestosis when demolishing a building, political anxieties, or missing a committee cycle. Sometimes legislative changes impose unpredicted and unpredictable additional costs. The Care Standards Act 2000 and the development of national standards for care are likely to increase overall costs significantly. Any plan has to be sufficiently robust to accommodate this and any financial modelling needs to be geared to the medium term not to a single year.

If the strategy is to be based on closures of in-house residential provision, it will be essential to identify separately the potential revenue savings and the capital expenditure which would be necessary to meet current standards. The revenue savings are not the same as the current running costs. First, current costs are likely to contain overheads – transport, maintenance, central costs for personnel, finance and support costs which may have to be redistributed. Second, some staff will have to be redeployed elsewhere. Third, redundancy costs need to be taken into account. The net saving may be less than half the current revenue costs at least until the building has been both vacated and sold.

If new services are to be developed through a competitive bidding process, there will be substantial transaction costs in preparing documentation and staff time. Willing the end does not finance the means to achieve that end. Budgetary provision needs to be made for the staff time and costs involved in handling that process. The commissioner in charge of the process needs to assess whether all the factors have been included and then add a substantial provision for contingencies.

Negotiation

Negotiating skills are essential. The complexity of the commissioning task will involve negotiations with health about the implications for future joint working. It will involve negotiations with a range of potential providers both to set out the preferred strategy of the authority and subsequently to test out the feasibility of providers meeting the service requirement. Financial awareness is particularly important in dealing with providers and needs to reflect the principles of fairness and openness discussed earlier.

What is negotiation? Is negotiation essentially confrontational echoing the definition of diplomacy as 'war carried on by another name' or is it a process designed to achieve a fair balance of interests between the parties? While the emphasis throughout this book is on the importance of trying to build consensus and working through collaboration to achieve objectives, it would be naïve to translate those principles to every negotiating situation. And each negotiating situation is different, so the approach needs to reflect that.

Negotiation is the process of discussion between two or more parties with different interests with a view to reaching an agreed position. In the case of Midshire, what negotiations will be involved for the strategic commissioner? Before a commissioning plan can be developed, there will be a process of negotiation with health colleagues. It may not be called negotiation but in essence it is a process of agreeing a shared position. This is now consolidated in the Joint Investment Plan required of health and local authorities but it is the result of discussions about the balance of expenditure between two systems which are interdependent. Every delayed discharge puts pressure on acute hospitals committed to difficult targets of reducing waiting lists, keeping down length of stay and maximizing throughput. Every long-stay geriatric bed closed or hospital-based respite care bed reduced puts pressure on social services both for increased residential care expenditure and for community support services. The two agencies have been drawn closer together particularly in relation to the care of older people by the range of joint initiatives required of them. The difficulties experienced with the continuing care agreements when first required are unlikely to recur.

When there is an external driver – for example, an agreed plan which has to be submitted to the Department of Health – consensus may be easier to achieve than if one authority is proposing unilaterally to reduce provision in a way which will have serious consequences for the other. Three conditions need to govern this set of circumstances which may occasionally be unavoidable because the budgeting cycles and budgetary pressures are different. First, give the maximum possible notice to colleagues in the other agency even as a pre-emptive warning before final decisions have been taken. Second, be prepared to explain in detail why this measure has had to be taken with appropriate facts, figures and costings. A third condition would be always look for ways of softening the impact of the change for colleagues either by phasing the implementation or offering to share some of the costs imposed on the other body for a limited period.

Negotiating with potential providers requires a different approach. What matters to the authority is the maintenance of good standards of service at an acceptable cost. The ways in which quality and pricing considerations can best be built into contractual arrangements have been discussed above. The strategic commissioner will be operating at an authority-wide level and has to have regard to the big picture. A deal with a provider in one locality has implications for the other localities both in terms of the total resource available and also in terms of the precedent set for other providers. Midshire may have political pressures encouraging transfer to a well-regarded local voluntary organization in one locality but that transfer has to be on no more favourable terms than those available to other providers. The grapevine is as active between providers as between commissioning authorities. The sharing of experience will be made more transparent under Best Value as a result of the benchmarking exercises carried out by commissioners.

Negotiation with providers whether before or after a tender process is likely to focus on cost. The issue may be one of quality but the area of discussion will be cost because there is a price attached to superior quality. That may be staffing levels required to secure the level of night-time cover necessary to meet inspection standards or to cover replacement costs for a staff development programme, the number of specialist baths available in the premises or the level of activities provided. Each has a price tag attached. One of the truisms of the construction industry is that contractors make their money not on the core contract price but on the charges they levy for the extras and variations inserted post-contract, and on the tortuous process of claims and counter-claims prior to the final settlement figure. Avoiding that process is highly desirable, so negotiating skills come into play.

The commissioner has to be clear about the importance of the issue under discussion – is it an essential without which the contract cannot go ahead, a highly desirable feature or a preference? The commissioner has to be clear about the maximum figure which they are willing to pay for the enhancement of service (it may be nothing, of course). That is the starting point for the discussion.

What skills will the commissioner need in the discussion to deliver the desired outcome? First, the commissioner will use powers of persuasion to explain the significance of the issue for the authority and the limited finance available. Second, there will be a threat (usually implied rather than real) of the withdrawal of the agreement if the provider fails to negotiate realistically. Third, there will be a flexibility in discussion. The starting point should not be the bottom line. As in an auction, one does not make one's first offer at the highest one is willing to go. Fourth, and part of that flexibility is a willingness to understand the provider's position and form a judgement on how far they are able to go in satisfying the purchaser's requirements. Mutual understanding is a critical element in successful negotiation.

Political sensitivity

One of the distinguishing features of local authority commissioning is the need for political sensitivity. The qualities needed for successful line management include clarity, determination and leadership. In dealing with politicians those qualities have their place but need to be accompanied by the softer skills of diplomacy and judgement. Many Directors have unexpectedly left their authorities as a result of their failure to read the political runes accurately.

In Midshire one can see a number of areas for political nervousness. These include the possible retreat from direct provision of residential care which will worry politicians because of the public attachment to homes as the visible expression of a caring community, and the rebalancing between localities which will create losers in some areas. Paradoxically, the new structure of local government may make it more difficult to achieve change than was intended by its creators. In the previous structure the necessity for approval required endorsement by the Social Services Committee. This meant that there was one individual – the Chair – and one Committee – the Social Services Committee – which had to be persuaded. The division between the Executive and the scrutiny roles means that one now has to persuade all members of the Executive and then withstand the sniping from the Scrutiny Committee which does not have the same ownership of the decision.

How can one develop political sensitivity? The first thing to understand is the policies of the majority group as expressed in any manifesto. The second is the politics of the Council. Where, as in Midshire the Council is hung, what are the key alliances? If there is a majority group, who are the key figures? How dominant is the leader? Is there an oppositional faction within the majority group? What are the issues on which there have been tensions previously? The third is the personal position of councillors. If homes are to close, whose wards are likely to be most affected? Does a councillor have particular links with a home, maybe as Chair of the Friends of the home? In other words, one needs to understand where opposition is likely to come from and why.

Understanding is essential but how can one sell a difficult policy choice? Information, information and information. Members need to be given all the information which has led to the recommendations for change including the unfair distribution of services, the costs of re-provision, the available finances to meet re-provision, the impact on local communities and the political risks involved. Commissioners need to anticipate the grounds where there may be political sensitivities and meet them head-on with facts not with argument.

If in Midshire a private residential care place can be purchased through the market at £220 per week, it is difficult to justify an in-house unit cost of £290 per week, especially so given the overall requirement to find savings. If alternative provision is available which meets the quality test (measured objectively if possible as suggested in Chapter 7), which meets the accessibility test in terms of being accessible by transport routes for relatives and friends of residents and enables the residents to maintain their social links, and this can be delivered with an overall revenue saving and a major saving on capital costs, one can begin to develop a case. And if the savings generated (or a portion of them) are to be ploughed back into the development of community-based support services including enhanced home care and respite provision, one has a very powerful set of facts with which to take on those resistant to change.

The most potent argument to be deployed is the support of users and carers for the direction of change. This cannot be achieved as a one-off exercise. Users and carers are rightly very sensitive to any suggestion of being made to dance to the purchasers' tune and acutely aware of the potential for manipulation of their views. But good practice should mean that some of the examples given in Chapter 3 are in existence, providing a regular forum for direct dialogue. The information available to councillors should always be made available to users and carers to help them bring their perspective to the discussion. It is these representatives – direct or indirect – of consumer interests who have the most immediate and acute investment in quality services. Securing their support for a radical shift which will improve quality is therefore a very powerful lever in addressing the politicians. If the collective support is not secured at an early stage, one runs the risk of opposition to change using the residents of the homes as an emotive argument for retention of the status quo.

ACTIVITY 2.1: WRITING A STRATEGIC PLAN

We have used the example of Midshire (see p. 21) to illustrate some of the issues facing strategic commissioners.

- Refer back to the facts set out earlier.
- Draw up a draft strategic commissioning statement for older people concentrating on how you would rebalance care both geographically and between residential and community-based services.
- Take into account the political constraints and ensure that the plan is financially robust.

JOINT COMMISSIONING

Joint commissioning is a concept which has been discussed for several years as a way of bridging the divide between health and social care. Examples of innovative ways of organizing the commissioning of care services are multiplying rapidly. Herefordshire has combined the posts of Chief Executive of the Health Authority and Director of Social Services to secure a coordinated approach to health and social care commissioning. The changes in the 1999 Health Act have given the discussion real impetus by removing some of the legislative barriers to pooling budgets and pooling authority. The potential for integrated working and the remaining problems in delivering this are discussed in detail in Chapter 8. Before looking at the specific skills required for joint commissioning in the fast-moving context of health and social care, it is important to acknowledge the scale of the inter-agency problems.

Health and social care continue to inhabit different worlds. The former is a centrally controlled service responding to priorities set by government at national level. It is wholly funded by taxpayers' money raised through National Insurance and the tax system. It is locally administered. It has had a surfeit of organizational changes in the past fifteen years as successive governments have wrestled with how best to improve quality and how to control costs. It is a service of provider power with doctors both in hospital settings and primary care having a dominant influence on how services are staffed and delivered. The political sensitivity of such issues as waiting lists and the pay of nurses means that the NHS is an issue in every election campaign. At the same time the NHS is riven with what in an industrial context would be termed restrictive practices with the Royal Colleges using their power of accreditation and control of training as a powerful lever against change, and the British Medical Association justifying its reputation as the most effective trade union.

By contrast, local authority social care is funded through local taxation even if nearly three-quarters of all its expenditure is supported by grants from central government. It is subject to local political control and locally determined priorities. Social services departments have existed for thirty years as the vehicle for delivering social care at a time when many other services including health, housing and education were undergoing radical change. The provider power exercised through the trade union movement in the 1970s and early 1980s has been substantially eroded. Commissioning has become the primary task of social services rather than the direct delivery of care.

The two services, although working together on many issues, are not natural partners. The differences in funding are compounded by different timed budgetary cycles although the planning cycles which used to be out of alignment have now been drawn closer together through the Health Improvement programme and other joint statements. The two services have in the past had very different approaches to the role of users and carers. Patients often ascribe God-like qualities to their consultants. Some consultants act as if they believe these fantasies! This relationship is very different to the user relationship with social care staff. It is not easily reconciled with the central role given to users and carers in the delivery of effective social care. Patients as partners is attractive rhetoric but rarely occurs in health care practice. The patient role is still predominantly that of the passive unquestioning recipient of treatment defined and delivered by others. That culture is beginning to change with scandals such as Alder Hey and Bristol driving the process but there is a long way to go before patients have the same level of influence and control over how they are treated as social care recipients.

The joint commissioner, whether from a health or social care background, needs to understand these cultural issues if they are to work successfully across the boundary lines. They also need to understand that the two services have developed their commissioning roles rather differently. The NHS was formally split between purchasing authorities – the Health Authority which has subsequently been required to devolve many of its purchasing functions to primary care groups and primary care trusts – and provider authorities in the form of NHS Trusts. The intention was to bring the disciplines of the market to bear on health care provision. The relationship was, if not openly confrontational, suspicious with purchasers seeking to drive down costs, look for better deals elsewhere, and setting demanding throughput targets. The advent of the Labour Government in 1997 replaced GP fundholding with primary care groups and heralded a new era of collaboration between commissioners and providers.

A commissioning process based on mutual mistrust was replaced by one in which both parties had access to all relevant information – called open-book negotiations.

The experience of commissioning in the NHS has therefore been that of commissioning acute care. It has been dominated by block contracts with large-scale providers. Extra-contractual referrals (ECRs) were the equivalent of spot purchasing individual remedies for patients with particular needs. Their escalating cost led health authorities to impose controls on such referrals as a means of controlling budgets. Commissioners worked with GPs to find cost-effective alternatives. In contrast, spot purchasing has been the dominant pattern in most social service departments with limited experience of block contracts.

The Health Act 1999 implemented the approach set out in the consultative paper *Partnership in Action* (Department of Health 1998). It introduced three mechanisms for the delivery of effective joint working. First, pooled budgets allow both health agencies and social services to bring resources together in a ring-fenced fund to pay for services. Instead of boundary disputes, agencies will agree the components of a coordinated care package and meet the costs from the pooled budget without worrying whether social care costs or health care costs are being met from the pool. In this way the pooled budget becomes a common resource equally accessible to both agencies.

Second, it provided for lead commissioning whereby the two agencies agree that one will take the lead responsibility for commissioning for a particular care group. The lead commissioner then commissions services for both agencies using their available agency budget to do so. The advantage is that it gives coordination of commissioning across the boundary while resources remain formally and legally within the control of the single agency. This is helpful in meeting political sensitivities about democratic control of public finances. It is thus less radical but arguably more readily achieved than pooled budgets.

Third, it provided for the introduction of integrated provision enabling professionals to work together in a single unified management structure. This integration can be under the control of one or other agency or a new integrated structure with distinctive management arrangements may be created. The new structure may be a direct provider, for example, drawing together all community support services for older people from district nurses to home helps, or it may contract with other providers to offer services to a care group or locality.

ACTIVITY 2.2: JOINT COMMISSIONING

You have been appointed as joint commissioner for services to people with disabilities. The local authority and Health Authority have a long history of poor relationships but new appointments at Director and Chief Executive level in the two authorities are generally seen as heralding a new era of cooperation. The decision to appoint a joint commissioner for these services has therefore symbolic importance. The snag is that no agreement has yet been reached on how to use the new flexibilities under the Health Act. Your first task is to review the position and recommend a model to the two authorities.

The Mental Health Trust opposed the remit of the post arguing that learning disabilities should be part of the new integrated trust which is being developed.

At present the Health Authority spends about £3 million on services for people with disabilities and the local authority about £2 million including a direct payments scheme for service users. An active user group is very hostile to the medical model of care. Both health and social services employ occupational therapists and there is great anxiety from both staff groups about radical change. How would you approach the task and what factors would influence your recommendation?

The 1999 Health Act represented a great leap forward but may itself be overtaken by the desire of ministers to push ahead more rapidly than the enabling framework of the Act would deliver. The National Health Service plan presaged the introduction of a new type of body – Care Trusts, which would draw together health and social care responsibilities, and the introduction of unified mental health trusts spanning both health and social care. Organic change may therefore be overtaken by enforced change.

One of the arguments long advanced against any model of integrated health and social care has been the dominance of the acute sector of care in the thinking of NHS managers and even more so of politicians. Waiting lists were one of Labour's key pledges in the 1997 election campaign and the NHS will remain a salient political issue for any government. The drive to integration stems from concern more about the impact of delayed discharges in adding to pressures on the acute sector than the quality of care delivered by the separate services. The touchstone of success may therefore be what happens in the acute sector rather than improvements in community care delivery. One wonders whether there is something awry in the decision-making process to produce this perverse indicator of success.

The joint commissioner therefore needs to be clear about the performance framework within which they are operating and to ensure that the performance targets against which any commissioning strategy is judged are (a) relevant to the service; and (b) within the control of the service.

Given the pace of change and the alternative structures which can be developed, it may be helpful to summarize the options and their advantages and disadvantages:

- *Single service commissioning*: this is the traditional way of commissioning. There may be problems in coordination with other agencies with different budget pressures and different priorities.

- *Coordinated commissioning*: two commissioners with independent budgets and priorities but with close liaison to secure complementary activities in care delivery. This can work well but is crucially dependent on personal relationships between the two commissioners.

- *Lead commissioning*: one commissioner who commissions for both agencies but with separate service budgets and lines of accountability within each agency. This preserves lines of accountability but enables the lead commissioner to take a single view of priorities.

- *Lead commissioning with pooled budget*: one commissioner with a single integrated budget. This gives a clear single view of priorities and shares resources. It requires a high level of mutual trust especially from the agency without any managerial control over the lead commissioner.

- *Single commissioner with a pooled budget working to Partnership Board*: the commissioner has one budget and one accountability line, albeit to a Board with joint representation from health and social care. It is unlikely that the Board will move to a single commissioner for all services. Many are likely to establish a single commissioner for one service but prefer to act in a more consultative role for other services.

Regardless of the structural arrangements in place, it is clear that there is a strong drive to secure closer integration of health and social care. The full implications of this and the changing nature of the social care market are addressed in the final chapter.

KEY POINTS

☐   Commissioning takes place at all levels of the organization.

☐   Care management describes a commissioning process for individuals.

☐   Strategic commissioning is the process of matching needs to resources in a way which secures equity and uses resources efficiently.

☐   Commissioning requires skills in analysis, negotiation, and political sensitivity.

☐   Joint commissioning will continue to grow in importance but needs to recognize the different structures and cultures of health and social care.

KEY READING

The Department of Health provides a good starting point for further reading. *An Introduction to Joint Commissioning* (1995a) and *Practical Guidance on Joint Commissioning for Project Leaders* (1995) set the context and offer helpful advice. The importance of operating within a market context is true across local government. The broader picture is well set out in *Public Services and Market Mechanisms* (1995) by Walsh. Hudson's *Making Sense of Markets in Health and Social Care* (1994) is a short book but with admirable clarity discusses the issues for commissioners. The best model for the fledgling commissioner is *Commissioning Mental Health Services* (1996) where Thornicroft and Strathdee set out the issues which commissioners need to reflect in their planning. The place of commissioning in the new world of local government is covered best by Corrigan, Hayes and Joyce in *Managing in the New Local Government* (1999). Although written in a health care context there is a very thoughtful analysis of new models in Light's *Effective Commissioning* (1998).

CHAPTER 3

INVOLVING USERS AND CARERS

OBJECTIVES

This chapter will help you to understand:

▦ Why the role of users and carers is so important in social care.

▦ How and when users and carers *must* be involved in the contracting process, and when it is desirable.

▦ What messages can be learned from the shift to direct payments.

▦ How you can adjust your practice to work in partnership with users and carers.

THE RIGHTS OF USERS AND CARERS

> Welfare is about rights, not caring. I do not want to live in the 'caring society', a nanny state in which the care we get depends on what the caring professions think fit for us to receive. I would much prefer to live in a society which struggles to be just, which respects and enhances people's rights and entitlements.
>
> (Ignatieff 1989)

That statement neatly encapsulates the social model of disability which has pioneered the attitudinal shift of the past twenty years in relation to service users.

The involvement of users and carers in the purchasing process is not an optional extra. It is one of the features which sharply separates contracting and purchasing social care from the same tasks in other services. The most striking shift in public policy on personal social services in the past twenty years has not been the introduction of new purchasing arrangements but the emphasis on users and carers. The carers movement brilliantly led by Jill Pitkeathley (now Baroness Pitkeathley) transformed the landscape by drawing the attention of key decision-makers to the toll on the lives of those in caring roles who went unsupported and unrecognized. This in turn influenced both the 1988 Griffiths Report and the 1990 NHS and Community Care Act. Subsequent legislation like the 1995 Carers (Recognition and Services) Act has further extended the rights of carers.

What is more recent is the emphasis in policy that service users have rights. They are not passive recipients of what the professionals believe is good for them. They have the right to challenge, to complain, to be heard and to be involved in their care plan. Twenty years ago they did not even have the right to see what was being written about them and to challenge its accuracy. And carers have rights to an assessment of their needs, to be involved in the construction of the care plan, and to be consulted about changes.

Often professionals link users and carers (this chapter does too) but it is always important to remember that the needs and priorities of the users and their carer may be very different as the next case study illustrates.

CASE STUDY 5: CONFLICTING RIGHTS

Mary B is a 72-year-old widow. When her husband died four years ago she asked her mother who was then 89 to come to live with her. Mary's mother had fallen a few weeks earlier and Mary was worried about her mother living alone in a rural village without easy access to help. Two years after moving in with Mary, her mother had a stroke and is now immobile and has continence problems. For Mary life has become a constant round of cooking, washing, feeding and cleaning. She feels at the end of her tether and badly needs a holiday but knows that there is nobody else to care for her mother who would have to go into a home while Mary is away. Her mother is terrified at the prospect of being 'put away'.

- What are Mary's needs?
- What are her mother's needs?
- Are they reconcilable?

Just as these two individuals have different priorities and needs, so too users and carers give a different perspective when involved in the commissioning and purchasing process.

THE SOCIAL MODEL OF DISABILITY

In understanding the user's perspective a little social theory is necessary. The disability movement has been the main driving force for change in the way in which professionals view users. The rights which have been secured were initially in the context of disability. It is helpful to illustrate the concept by comparing the social model of disability and the medical model.

The traditional medical model sees disability as a handicap with which the disabled person has to come to terms, helped by professionals who will help to define their needs and provide appropriate care and support for those needs. Care management is a process rooted in that traditional model of assessment. It is carried out by professionals who define need in their terms and, subject to eligibility criteria, offer an appropriate care package to meet those needs.

In contrast, the social model of disability focuses on 'the oppression which people with physical, sensory or intellectual impairments, or those who are mental health survivors, experience as a result of prejudicial attitude and discriminatory actions. People are disabled by society's reaction to impairment' (Morris 1993: x). To the list cited by Morris one might add older people where the same prejudiced attitudes apply and those from ethnic minorities where the discrimination and prejudice are most blatant.

The social model emphasizes the personal assistance necessary for disabled people to participate in all the activities of everyday life. These includes work, leisure pursuits, education and personal relationships. It aims to maximize the choice and control which disabled people can exercise in making decisions, both about their personal assistance and the activities in which they wish to participate. Choice means a real choice over where to live, how to live, and who provides assistance and control over how, when and what assistance is offered. This is a frontal assault on the professional prescription of what needs to be done and presents a huge challenge to social care in struggling to integrate this degree of choice and control within existing structures.

The social model stresses rights. 'To be disabled in Great Britain is to be denied the fundamental rights of citizenship to such an extent that most disabled people are denied their basic human rights' (Oliver 1993). It rejects the concept of care, preferring the role of cash in improving the quality of life of those with disabilities. By emphasizing the maximum possible choice and control, it rejects any stigmatizing services and the dominance of the assessment model whereby professionals determine the lifestyle and choices of others.

This description of the social model immediately throws up a latent tension with the priorities of carers. This is most evident in the care of people with learning disabilities. Parents who have carried total responsibility for the upbringing of their child are sometimes very reluctant to see their vulnerable child exposed to a more risky environment of a hostel or group home. Who has choice and control? At what point does the impairment of an individual limit their capacity to take effective control of their lives? In the example above the priorities of Mary and her mother were different, their choices would be different.

But many of the service characteristics which the social model would champion are also the priorities of carers – dignity, safety and security, reliability. The insights which both users and carers can bring to the commissioning and purchasing process are an important counter-balance to the views of professionals who often tend to view the world in organizational rather than human terms.

THE SPECTRUM OF INVOLVEMENT

The views of users and carers need to be sought at all stages of the commissioning process from the micro-commissioning of care management through to the strategic commissioning across the authority as whole. There is a wide range of involvement which needs to be explored.

Table 3.1 shows how different techniques are needed for consultation than are used when user control is on the agenda. The spectrum is not one of right or wrong because work needs to proceed at a pace with which user and carers groups are comfortable. Where possible, the goal should be to move to the right-hand side of the spectrum as and when users are ready to do so. The techniques on the left-hand side are often the necessary starting point both to secure engagement and to develop the confidence of service users.

Table 3.1 The spectrum of involvement

Consultation	Participation	Control
User surveys	Users on committees	Users selecting contractors
Focus groups	User advisory groups	Users selecting staff
Consultation meetings		Users managing services

The Joint Review process which has now been used by the Audit Commission and Social Services Inspectorate for five years adopts the relatively blunt instrument of a client survey to assess overall user satisfaction with the services which they are receiving. This does, however, provide a good indicator of the quality of provision. Far more use could be made of client surveys to refine the planning process. The requirement through Best Value to extend the role of consultation makes it likely that they will be increasingly influential in refining and developing policy. Such surveys can go far beyond assessments of the quality of meals on wheels. They do, however, require agencies to put the same kind of investment into market research that would be true of commercial enterprises, and to develop skills in survey design that currently are rarely found in the public sector.

Focus groups are a useful way of eliciting user views on a specific topic. A pure method would seek to get a cross-section of the target population reflecting age, ethnicity, class and gender, but this is often unrealistic and unnecessary. Even the blunt instrument of getting together a group with a shared interest in the topic can be helpful in rounding out the data which may have come from the survey.

If the survey showed a high level of dissatisfaction with the front desk reception and telephone response, a focus group could be used to identify the specific problems and to establish the user perspective on the type of reception service they would wish to have. It is unthinkable that a Best Value review should be undertaken without some structured form of consultation with users. The Department of Health guidance to the performance assessment framework said:

> Meaningful consultation can make services more responsive and can also increase public confidence in those services. In developing targets for the cost and quality of services to deliver Best Value, local authorities will be expected to consult widely with the local community.
>
> (Department of Health 1999)

Departments have moved on from the naïve belief that copies of the Community Care Plan in the public library could be regarded as consultation even where these are supported by public meetings and translations into minority languages. This is an inadequate response to the task of reaching out to those users usually unresponsive to conventional consultation. Working through outreach staff based in or supporting minority groups can give valuable insights into the barriers which prevent full engagement. Working through faith-based groups can be useful, especially with Muslim communities, in helping staff of public authorities to understand how best to communicate with minority groups.

The messages will differ between different care groups and different localities but the consultation process, whenever it has been undertaken, shows remarkable consistency in highlighting common preoccupations from service users. These include:

- *Accessibility of services*: this means physical access to conveniently located offices near major transport routes which do not have stairs to limit access for older people, young mothers with children and disabled people. It also means friendly reception facilities, information readily available in a variety of formats and a sense from the moment one crosses the threshold that this is an environment which values its users and treats them decently.

- *Reliability*: this means being confident that services or assistance will arrive when promised, and will do so on time. It means confidence that the same worker will turn up and, if not, that the user will be notified in advance of the change. This is important in giving freedom to people to organize their own lives without being dependent on the fluctuating arrival times of any helper.

- *Safety and security*: when 'bogus social workers' were first mentioned in the media it seemed implausible. Who would want to identify themselves in this way? Sadly it is all too real a fear for housebound elderly people trapped in their own homes, dependent on support from others and vulnerable to crime. In the context of safety and security it is important for users to know who will visit and at what time. These basic issues are too often given scant attention by service planners but are critical. Continuity of the individual delivering care is an undervalued priority for many professionals in the delivery of care.

- *Flexibility*: this is not a quality traditionally associated with public sector services. The domination of provider interests and the rigidity of bureaucratic systems militate against the flexibility needed to deliver individually responsive services. Even where user views are taken into account, the response is an organizational systems response rather than an individualized service. Yet it is that individualization of care which gives dignity to service users and to carers. Treating users as individual people with their own name and not just as a day centre member, or meal on wheel recipient, is what those commissioning should require from providers. All too often staff in homes and in hospitals use first names when talking to older people without having sought their permission and without any sensitivity to this further erosion of dignity. In a hotel it would be Mrs Brown and Mr Black. One cannot always prescribe these quality issues in a contract but one can require the establishment of resident committees or other relevant user groups. The inescapable imbalance of power especially in the residential context may limit the effectiveness of these groups but they can be strengthened through independent advocacy support if necessary.

- *Choice*: the statutory Direction on choice gives a theoretical right to users to choose their residential placement. In reality, the choice is more circumscribed by finance – the area may not have homes available at a price the authority is willing to pay – and by other pressures. Delayed discharges have become the touchstone of NHS efficiency and the patient refusing to move from an acute bed because no residential or nursing home place meets their preferences is likely to come under a great deal of pressure, both overt and covert, from NHS staff. Choice, however, goes more widely than residential care. It covers the whole range of provision. The mixed economy has helped to shift providers, public and private, from a one size fits all approach, but there is still far to go before the service is wholly responsive to individuals.

- *Control*: when disability, mental ill health or ageing limit the possibilities of fully independent living, they affect the ability of the service user to be in control of their life. This loss of control is felt keenly. This is why the disability movement has placed such emphasis on putting users in control of their lives to the fullest degree possible. This includes control over who is employed to assist them, when that assistance is offered and how that assistance is offered. The phrase empowerment is used to describe the conscious attempt by workers to give control and power back to users. But the demand for control not only requires flexibility from the service provider but can also pose difficult ethical issues.

  How far can the provider be expected to go to meet the wishes of the service user? For example, is it reasonable for a user to have the right to ask for a change of worker? Should that request be met unconditionally and repeatedly or is there a limit to the degree of user control? If the reason given for the change is that a white user wants a white worker, is that acceptable? If an Asian client wants an Asian worker, is that acceptable? If a Protestant in North Belfast wants a Protestant worker, is that acceptable? The application of anti-discriminatory practice and values is a sound guide but these issues do require careful thought and careful explanation to users.

The themes of accessibility, flexibility, reliability, safety, choice and control are recurrent. The task of the commissioner is to ensure that they are reflected in commissioning practice at all levels, and that the users' and carers' perspectives inform decision-making throughout the agency. Use the next case study to assess how fully they were reflected in the example described.

CASE STUDY 6: LISTENING TO USERS

A local authority decided to tender its home care service, dividing its service between practical and personal care. External suppliers won the contract for practical care (shopping and cleaning) which was split into three geographical areas each with different providers. Personal care was retained in-house. Many users whose needs were not defined as personal care (bathing, toileting, etc.) lost their previous worker as the new providers took over.

Between the tender process and the start of the contract one of the successful bidders was taken over by a major national non-profit provider with a well-established reputation. The initial weeks of the contract were disastrous. Roster systems did not work. Different workers turned up each day to users' homes. The barrage of complaints became deafening. After several warnings the local authority terminated the contract and had to take over the service itself.

A further change of worker ensued before the local authority decided to split the contract between the two other providers which had performed reasonably well. Another change of worker therefore followed. The upshot was that an authority which tendered to secure savings ended up making no savings and showing scant regard for the service users in the process. Some users had up to five different workers in a three-month period.

- Could the user views have been built into the contracting process?
- Were the problems avoidable?
- Would a user advisory group have produced a different outcome?

FROM CONSULTATION TO PARTICIPATION

Consultation is an ongoing process. Surveys can be even more valuable in measuring change over time than in giving a snapshot picture. An organization committed to continuous improvement needs to be able to test whether it is making progress and asking the same questions every year can give a real sense of the direction of travel to the organization. An organization committed to listening to its users might therefore be expected to have:

- an annual survey measuring overall satisfaction with the performance of the particular service or department
- focus groups of users and non-users to explore problem areas identified from the survey
- consultation groups of users and carers to discuss new ideas and developments at locality and area-wide level

CASE STUDY 7: BETTER GOVERNMENT FOR OLDER PEOPLE

A local authority was selected as a pilot area for the Better Government for Older People initiative. It engaged on an extensive programme of consultation with service users, community groups, senior citizens clubs, minority groups and others. It found that its previous consultation exercises which had followed the traditional route of full documents in the library, summaries to every household including summaries of the summary in minority languages and public meetings in different parts of the authority had completely failed to reach the majority of its older citizens. The language used was impenetrable and the Civic logo on a document made most people throw it away. As part of its programme under Better Government for Older People it established an older people's reading group. This was not to study the literary merits of Jane Austen but to ensure that all council documents intended for the public were clear, concise and comprehensible. It achieved the dual objective of improving the standard of the council's material and also giving a sense of ownership and pride to the older people involved.

This example is an illustration of the move along the continuum from consultation to participation. By working on a consistent basis with groups of users and carers it is possible to change the culture of the authority so that user participation moves from the margin to the mainstream.

A necessary starting point is a regular forum in which users can meet. This can be facilitated by the authority but should not be run by it. It will need to establish a committee and officers but does not initially need the formality of a constitution. The key factor is that it should clearly be owned by users and constitute a forum in which they can have their say without fear. That means there should be a minimum of professional staff present at the meetings. Professionals underestimate the degree to which their presence can inhibit others, especially when they are present in some numbers. Above all, it means that those staff who are present have to avoid defensiveness in explaining away any identified shortcomings in service.

It is inevitable that service users feel anxious about expressing criticism. Their vulnerability and dependence on social care support mean that they are often fearful of upsetting 'the powers that be' and are consequently loath to criticize. The first task of the facilitator, and most groups will need one at least initially, is to create a confident environment in which views can be frankly expressed. But to get the best out of any such forum it will need to move beyond a vehicle for complaints and grumbles and become a vehicle for sharing ideas for development. Here the onus has to shift to senior managers in the department to be ready to bring proposals for discussion before they are finalized.

This shift is easier said than done. The tradition of local government is that proposals for change only come into the public arena after detailed internal discussion, costing and scrutiny. Officers are very nervous that embryo ideas could be stillborn if they are discussed prematurely and leaked to the local press by those opposed to any change. Involving users in shaping proposals so that when they emerge publicly they are acceptable and indeed welcomed by users is a major cultural shift for both officers and members.

ACTIVITY 3.1: MINIMIZING RISK

The department has recently established a Senior Citizens Consultative Group. The Director takes to the group before discussion with the Social Services Committee the initial findings of an internal review which suggests that the authority is over-reliant on residential care. It recommends the transfer or closure of the majority of its provision and reinvestment in improved domiciliary care services and resource centres as an alternative.

- What could go wrong?
- What steps could be taken by the Director to minimize the risk?

GETTING USERS INVOLVED IN DECISIONS

Following through this example it is likely that the initial views of users to any extension of private services through the contracting process may well be hostile. The public sector does provide a level of reassurance to users about standards of care.

In addition to providing factual evidence of comparative costs and quality to reassure the users and carers groups, they could be asked to take part in the selection of contractors. It is always good practice to have an independent person on any selection panel and involving users directly in this way has several benefits. First, it makes it clear to potential contractors that the department takes the users' views seriously. Second, it is likely to improve the quality of decision-making by safeguarding against any prejudices on the part of the panel. Third, it introduces a different perspective by putting quality of care issues at the forefront. Fourth, it offers an opportunity to test the contractors' experience of work with users by seeing their response to the panel process.

Users can thus participate in policy formation at the consultation stage, in working out detail through local forums or committees and in the actual selection of contractors. The principle of involving users in appointments is one that can also be applied to residential and day care staff, and to fieldworkers. Many departments can take the first step by having users on appointments and interviewing committees for residential staff but are reluctant to extend that same principle to fieldwork. Yet it is essential that a social worker or care manager possesses good interpersonal skills which users would be well placed to evaluate and test.

The difficulties involved in bringing users into the recruitment process can be exaggerated. Macadam and Townsley, writing in the context of learning difficulties, describe some of the barriers to involvement as:

- Lack of guidance or training materials.
- Lack of commitment from managers.
- Opposition from trade unions and personnel departments.
- Lack of flexibility within established recruitment procedures.
- Doubts by staff and service managers about the ability of people with learning difficulties to be objective, maintain confidentiality and keep to equal opportunities practice.
- Lack of available training for service users in recruitment and fair selection procedures.

(1998: 208)

The gains, however, from overcoming these obstacles were real for the users and for the process itself. It demonstrated the culture of the service. It also demonstrated whether the candidates were able to relate to people with learning difficulties. 'The question "why do you want to work with us?" requires a clearer and more direct answer than why do you want this job?' (ibid.: 207). It served to discourage unsuitable candidates. And it was an empowering experience for the service users themselves. If it can be done successfully with people with learning difficulties, the argument for applying the approach with other client groups is overwhelming.

Effective user involvement has two key preconditions. First, it requires the commitment of managers in the service and, second, a readiness to invest time and resources to ensure that users can play a full part in the recruitment process and not be there as token members of the panel.

What this section of the chapter has covered is the shift in attitudes required to facilitate participation. Being responsive to the needs of service users means 'they are going to have to involve them and their supporters in all aspects of services' (Simons 1998: 266). Simons offers examples of user involvement:

> Hackney Social Services Department established four focus groups with a remit to look closely at different aspects of local services. Each focus group consisted of five or six people with learning difficulties, three or four carers and two or three professionals including colleagues from other agencies. Each group met a number of times, carried out visits to services and produced their own reports. These individual reports were then used to develop the community care plan.
>
> When the contract for a local day service came to an end, local purchasers (Avon Health Authority) worked with the previous provider to find ways to include people with learning difficulties in the reselection process. A representative of the local People First group was co-opted to the tender selection panel, as were four users of the existing service with their supporters . . . the process of selection (which included presentations by all the tendering organisations along with 'taster workshops') was designed to be both fair to the potential providers and accessible to the people with learning difficulties involved. So for example instant photographs were taken at each stage to remind members of the panel about the different options.
>
> (ibid.: 288)

TAKING CONTROL THROUGH DIRECT PAYMENTS

We have seen that control over their own lives is what people with disabilities want. That applies to other service users. Can that control be extended to control over services through the development of user-managed provision? The example of direct payments is important for it represents a breakthough in the way in which public sector agencies relate to people with disabilities, and the principle is capable of wider extension.

The Community Care (Direct Payments) Act 1996 makes it possible for people with disabilities to receive a payment from the local authority to pay for the services they require directly without the local authority taking responsibility for providing those services which it has assessed are needed by the person with disabilities. The payment can only be made where the authority is satisfied that the person has an assessed need under the community care legislation. Local authorities have to decide which needs can be met through a direct payment and which group of those with disabilities are eligible. Despite the inevitable bureaucracy attached to the introduction of a new scheme it is a real transfer of power from professionals to users.

The service user can use the money to buy or organize the type of support service which suits them best. They control the balance of time and support available, how and when it is available, and who is employed to deliver it. While the scheme is not mandatory and is within the discretion of local authorities, there has been a gradual increase in the number of areas with such schemes, whether paid directly to users or in some instances channelled through a Centre for Independent Living.

These centres offer back-up and support to users wanting to make their own arrangements for personal assistance. Service brokerage schemes whether through Centres for Independent Living or some other vehicle are important in winning support for direct payments. The responsibilities of employing people can be daunting. Brokerage can help those on direct payments through the necessary steps, can offer advice on the options available, and can support people through the implementation process and secure the quality standards they can reasonably expect from personal assistance.

Early research indicates that the personal care being purchased through direct payments includes both health and social care (Glendinning *et al.* 2000). It therefore achieves a policy objective of central government in securing an integrated package of support. Over 3,600 people were using direct payments in summer 2000 although 20 per cent of local authorities had no scheme in place (*Community Care*, 19 October 2000b: 5).

CASE STUDY 8: DIRECT PAYMENTS

John is a 23-year-old Afro-Caribbean man who is deaf and blind. He went to a special school and on leaving the school moved into rented accommodation with help from specialist staff. He has a good level of intelligence and is able to communicate both through direct contact on the palm and through the use of a computer screen. He is fiercely independent and resists any patronizing intervention from voluntary organizations or from social services.

- Would you consider John for a direct payments scheme?
- What kind of support might he require?
- What do you see as the obstacles in utilizing direct payments for John?

A suggested response to these questions is given in Chapter 9.

The principle of direct payments has now been extended to older people. Although the numbers eligible are much greater, the pace of take-up in the first years of the extension has been very slow. This is illustrative of some of the difficulties which have been experienced in the roll-out of the direct payments scheme:

- There is little information readily available about direct payments in areas where there is not an active advocacy group or a Centre for Independent Living.
- Where the information is available it is rarely accessible in the variety of formats needed for people with disabilities – Braille, cassettes, large format, Makaton, etc.
- Local authorities which have started schemes have concentrated on what may be termed the easy end of the market – people who have physical disabilities but whose intellectual capacities and speech are unaffected. The Act, however, applies more widely.
- Successful schemes need investment from the local authority in terms of providing support to those wishing to use direct payments either through providing advice and assistance with setting up a scheme or by funding brokerage or advocacy organizations.

A similar picture exists in relation to the extension to older people where the limited expressed demand for such a scheme may be used as a reason for inaction. The task of the commissioner is to go beyond this by using the techniques of advocacy which have more frequently been used in relation to those from ethnic backgrounds and the disabled. Older people can be socially excluded by prejudices deeply inlaid in society. Advocacy can help to redress the balance by giving expression to the views of older people themselves and giving them the support and confidence to express their views. Older people need to be involved in shaping the scheme but, above all, care managers have to be committed to the concept to encourage take-up by older people. Anti-discriminatory theory and the rhetoric of empowerment need to be translated into practice. Traditional social work skills can be utilized to empower the marginalized members of society.

Direct payments are one way in which service users can take direct control over their lives. But there are also ways in which the contribution of people with direct experience as users of services can be brought into the policy mainstream. These include Users Committees acting in an advisory role which could review and put forward comments on papers going to the Social Services Committee. While it may be argued that this is less significant than direct participation in decision-making through a co-opted member, sadly it has proved very difficult for co-opted members to have a major impact in politically polarized authorities. Often a solitary representative of users or carers, while listened to respectfully, has little real impact. A full committee of users and carers, even if designated advisory, can have a more powerful influence. Giving real influence to a body of this kind is indicative of the culture change which is essential if service users are to be at the centre of the evolving picture of social care provision.

User-managed services may be the next step forward as a logical extension of the direct payments principle. The active User and Carers Network in Wiltshire has developed this approach and is committed to giving users real control over their lives and futures. In local authorities there are many obstacles in the way of achieving the development of user-managed provision. First, the user-led organization is not likely to meet the test of financial stability for contractors when checked with Dun and Bradstreet. Second, by definition they are unlikely to be able to demonstrate the track record of successful delivery which purchasers like to see. Third, the requirement in Best Value to test services by competition may militate against locally based services which invest time and resources in developing high quality support services. The trade-off between cost and quality is ever present. Finally, the Performance Assessment

Framework set of performance indicators is currently more geared to inputs and unit costs than outcomes in terms of quality of life for service users which are more difficult to quantify.

This goes to the heart of the challenge to current practice. How can commissioners and purchasers hone their skills to work within a context of rights when their statutory base laid down in the NHS and Community Care Act is about professional assessment, packages of care and cost ceilings?

It is natural for professionals to be anxious about greater involvement from users. Users may challenge current approaches. They may generalize from their personal experience. They may seek to bring about changes to improve their personal situation rather than the position of all users. They may slow down the pace of the meeting. Many concepts readily understood by the professional will need to be explained to users.

All of this may be true in some instances. Just as new councillors have an induction programme and do not jump fully fledged into the arcane world of points of order and references back, so too service users need preparation and support if they are to move into greater involvement in meetings. This means that the organization as a whole as well as individual practitioners has to be committed to the process. Any group taking in service users for the first time has to have an opportunity to talk through the process and how members feel about it. Service users need to have the chance to meet members of the group individually rather than being thrust into a meeting room for first introductions.

The language used is important. Professionals live in a world of acronyms and jargon. These need to be excised from the discussion if possible or at least carefully explained. The 'keep it simple, stupid' message is essential and a good discipline for those whose stock in trade is the antithesis of clarity and conciseness.

Listening is a core social care skill. It is even more important when working with users in a group context. That does not mean patronizing users and investing their remarks with more attention than they would normally receive. It means treating their contributions with courtesy, finding positive links to the discussion and picking up comments made in any summary of the discussion. Sometimes, dependent on the nature of the difficulty experienced by the service user, it may be helpful for them to have a supporter available 'helping the person to get to the meeting on time, checking that they have the right papers, helping them read and digest papers before the meeting, and reinforcing and developing the service user's group discussion skills' (Whittaker 1993: 315).

Now let's see if we can put those principles into action.

ACTIVITY 3.2: PROMOTING USER INVOLVEMENT

You have just been appointed as service manager for people with disabilities in an urban unitary authority. You are responsible for three hostels for people with learning disabilities, and a number of satellite group homes. You oversee the work of the community team drawing health and social care professionals working with learning disabilities. There is an active Mencap group running evening and weekend activities. Day care is provided through a Social Education centre with increasing links with the Education department.

There is no direct service for people with physical disabilities although they are present in the two multi-purpose day centres which specialize in craft work, art and other activities.

Two wheelchair-bound women have approached the department pressing for the early introduction of a direct payments scheme.

While the department in its Community Care plan refers to the important role of users and carers, their involvement is currently limited to an annual meeting with the Director, the chance to comment on the draft community care plan and occasional 'what would you think if . . .' meetings on proposed new developments.

- What would you do to secure greater user involvement in the delivery of social care?
- Where would you start?
- What problems do you anticipate in bringing about change?
- How would you sell the idea to staff who were resistant or nervous about changes in their practice?
- How would you evaluate whether you had succeeded?

The delivery of community care services is constrained by the legislative framework – the 1990 NHS and Community Care Act – within which those services have to be delivered. But the tyranny of assessment can be broken by the culture shift advocated in this chapter. That means relying on users' self-assessment unless that assessment is so much at variance with the reality of what is available through public services as to be unreasonable. It means questioning arbitrary cost ceilings where the gains in quality of life and self-respect for the user can be demonstrated and quantified. It means a deliberate effort to transfer power over decision-making at every stage of the process from professionals to users. This is the essence of anti-discriminatory practice because, in Ignatieff's words at the beginning of this chapter, it is about 'a society which struggles to be just, which respects and enhances people's rights and entitlements'. It shifts the professional role to genuinely one of enabling by freeing those best placed to know their needs to articulate them and have the resources to acquire the services to meet those needs.

KEY POINTS

- ☐   The social model of disability is about rights.
- ☐   Users and carers need to be involved as much as they wish.
- ☐   The spectrum of involvement runs from consultation through participation to control.
- ☐   Direct payments are a way for users to take control over their lives.
- ☐   Anti-discriminatory practice is central to the task of working with users and carers.

KEY READING

Morris, *Independent Lives: Community Care and Disabled People* (1993) and Oliver, *Disability Citizenship and Empowerment* (1993) provide excellent introductions to the social model of disability. Ward's book, *Innovations in Advocacy and Empowerment* (1998) has some excellent case examples of translating the principles of empowerment into practice. Walker and Warren provide an interesting example of empowering older people in *Changing Services for Older People* (1996); Simons has written about involving people with learning disabilities in Ward's text and most pertinently in *A Seat at the Table: Involving People with Learning Disabilities in Commissioning and Purchasing Services* (1999).

CHAPTER 4

CARE MANAGEMENT

OBJECTIVES

By the end of this chapter you should be able to:

▦   Understand the crucial role played by the care manager.

▦   Identify the components of a comprehensive assessment.

▦   Understand what constitutes a care plan.

▦   Know what skills are required to act as a care manager.

THE DEVELOPMENT OF CARE MANAGEMENT

Residential care was the child of the Poor Law. Until very recently residential homes were sometimes located in former workhouses and carried a residual element of stigma. Social care workers had an inbuilt hostility to the residential model, weaned as they had been on Goffman's work on the destructive impact of institutionalization on the personality (Goffman 1962). The organizational structure of social services departments further reinforced the sense of residential care as the poor relation. The training, status and salary levels of residential workers were markedly inferior to those of fieldwork. Yet the social security changes explained in Chapter 1 meant that the numbers of people in residential care were growing rapidly. The Wagner Report on residential care argued:

> People who move into a residential establishment should do so by positive choice . . . There need to be real and valid alternatives on offer . . . there is no valid choice if people are driven into a residential establishment because domiciliary services are skimpy.
>
> (Wagner 1988: 7–8)

The reality was that home care services had developed as an afterthought to the primary welfare services for the elderly and were nowhere available in the range and volume to constitute a realistic alternative. A pilot was therefore necessary to test how far such an intensive service could be a substitute for residential care.

The concept of case management had been the subject of extensive research by the Personal Social Services Research Unit (PSSRU) at the University of Kent since the early 1980s. They provided the basis on which Griffiths was able to develop a critique of community care services as they existed in the mid-1980s. The Unit looked at the possibility of substituting community-based care for residential care, and identified scope for increasing the efficiency of care delivery.

Earlier findings on domiciliary care had shown that:

- There is a trade-off in the use of resources between intensity (a high level of input to households receiving a service measured in service hours) and cover (a service reaching a high proportion of the target population).
- Where authorities had increased expenditure on home care, this had been to achieve greater cover with a diminution of service intensity.
- Once a referral had been accepted, there was little variation in the pattern of delivery which did not reflect different needs.
- There was no correlation between high levels of elderly in the population and high expenditure – astonishingly the reverse was true.

(Davies and Challis 1986)

These gloomy findings on home care were the backdrop to the pilot study for it was evident that a radically different approach was required to ensure that resources were used effectively. The model which they tested was simple – the possibility of substituting community-based care for residential care by making available resource set at two-thirds the level of average residential care costs. By allocating a cash sum direct to the case manager it was hoped to break through the inflexibilities evident in the delivery system for community care. A number of local authorities were selected with different political control, different social characteristics and differing organizational arrangements. The impact of the studies on professional opinion was important although the evidence was as persuasive on the inefficiencies within the system as the evidence of improved outcomes. Reflecting on the range of projects studied including parallel work in the USA, the Netherlands and Australia, the PSSRU authors concluded:

- The implementation of the PSSRU model could greatly improve outcomes for clients measured by improved morale, better quality of life and reduced strain on carers.
- The model could achieve these outcomes at no greater costs.
- Case management costs were significant in relation to the sums spent on care support ranging from 19 to 29 per cent of total expenditure going on the assessment and management process.
- Administrative models of care management with non-professional staff with higher caseloads could be less expensive but could miss the essential skills in interagency working.

(Davies et al. 1990)

The conclusions of the studies were that the delivery of social care could be considerably improved by:

1   Clear and continuing case responsibility.
2   Targeted caseloads.
3   Smaller caseloads.
4   Trained and experienced fieldworkers.
5   Decentralised budget with clear expenditure limits.
6   Knowledge of the unit cost of services.
7   Costed service packages.
8   Systematic records for assessment and monitoring.
9   Closer health care linkages both formal and informal.

(Challis *et al.* 1993)

From this work PSSRU went on to develop different organizational models to deliver case management. This work was distinguished by the quality and detail of the analysis. It was extremely influential within the Department of Health and served to shape the future structures for the delivery of care management. In its guidance on care management the Department emphasized the assessment function, the need for clear eligibility criteria, the development of services based on the needs of individuals, the involvement of users and carers in the process of care planning and the assembly of a package of care services.

In the previous chapter the development of care management was linked to the recommendations in the Griffiths Report (1988). These clearly set out the proposed role for social services authorities.

> They should seek to negotiate the best possible prices for individual places in residential and nursing home care, reflecting the particular care needs of the individual concerned and local market conditions. They should look rigorously at the costs of comparable domiciliary services . . . And seek out the most efficient services there too, whether from the private voluntary or statutory sectors.
>
> (Griffiths Report 1988: 21)

This strategic role is discussed further in the chapters on commissioning and contracting. The Report, however, also spelt out how this would apply at the point of delivery. Where a significant amount of public resources was being applied to the care of an individual, a person should be appointed as a care manager to oversee the process of assessment and reassessment and to manage the process. The person would be expected to have accurate knowledge of the costs of providing different packages of care. There was a short-lived semantic argument about whether the task should be case or care management. Care management prevailed and that model with a designated care manager has remained as the primary vehicle for delivering planned and managed care.

089397

THE COMPONENTS OF CARE MANAGEMENT

The core elements of care management are:

- publishing and providing information
- receiving referrals and determining priorities
- assessing need
- care planning
- implementation of care plan
- monitoring
- evaluating and reviewing

This is expressed diagrammatically in Figure 4.1.

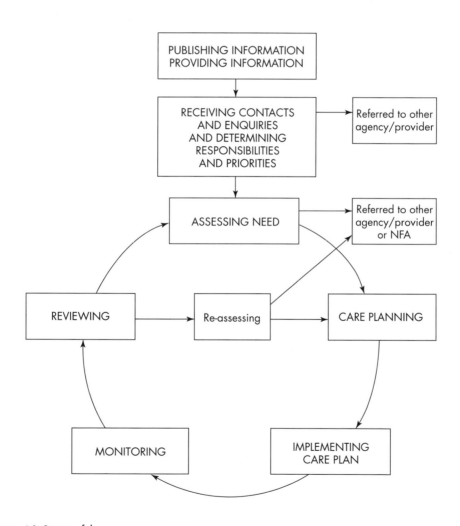

Figure 4.1 Stages of the care management process

Although assessment and care planning have become the dominant aspects of direct work with service users, it is important to take a rounded view of the care management process and include the functions of information giving and case screening as essential precursors to assessment.

Information

Improving the quality and accessibility of information about social services has been a priority. The criteria for services and the way in which assessments are carried out are readily available. Users are told of their right to see information held about them, including the care plan. The right to be heard and the right to complain without it being held against the complainant have all been achieved. Experiments galore have taken place in order to rid leaflets of jargon. Cartoon strips, the Plain English campaign and video technology have been used effectively.

It is essential to have information in a variety of formats so that it is available to as many as possible. Braille, large formats, cassettes, minority languages have all been used to communicate. The philosophy is simple – the provision of information is one way in which people can take control of their decision-making with full knowledge of the choices open to them.

Receiving referrals and establishing priorities (screening)

Social services departments receive thousands of calls each week. Some require action but many can be dealt with over the phone by sympathetic redirection to another agency. Social security offices and social services are a frequent source of confusion to users. Many queries also come to social services which are about housing needs and can possibly be dealt with more appropriately by housing departments.

The importance of the initial contact in shaping users' perception cannot be overstated. Reception staff are the unsung heroes and heroines of social services. They sometimes have to deal with clients who may be difficult, distressed and aggressive. A calm and unruffled response sets the tone for future work with the client. Treating people in a way which demonstrates respect for them as individuals helps their sense of self-worth and dignity.

Getting accurate information about the basics – name, address, post code if known, and accurate recording of the issue presented – is fundamental. In many offices this initial screening will be carried out by the reception staff. They will judge on the basis of the initial request for help whether an assessment is required. In busy urban offices a specialist duty team will cover all aspects of the initial contact. It is always better to err on the side of further work because that can subsequently be aborted if necessary. A failure to refer on somebody with a real need can be disastrous, losing an opportunity to get help to an individual at a critical time. For example, mental health referrals and particularly self-referrals do not always come with a clearly defined request but should always be referred for an assessment.

Assessment

Assessment has developed as the core function in many social services departments with a differentiation between a simple assessment for those presenting with a single need, and a complex assessment where more than one need was evident and more than one service or agency is involved in responding to that need.

CASE STUDY 9: A SIMPLE ASSESSMENT

Mrs G, a 79-year-old widow, is on the waiting list for a hip replacement. At an outpatient visit, she mentions that she is having difficulty in getting up after using the lavatory. Otherwise she is able to cope well in her bungalow. She is referred by the nurse at the outpatient clinic to social services requesting help with a raised toilet seat. The occupational therapist visits, confirms that Mrs G is an otherwise fit and healthy woman with no other need and proceeds to order supply and fit the seat. The OT suggests that Mrs G should contact the department again if her situation deteriorates or if she no longer needs the seat following her hip replacement.

The learning points of this case study are:

- The need to check out and validate the initial referral, and in particular to see if there are any other difficulties – social, financial or emotional – in Mrs G's situation. Those who have lost a partner are vulnerable to depression.
- The need to make arrangements for future contact, ideally with a named person.
- The need to make arrangements for the return of an aid when no longer required – social services recovery record on aids is very poor and many resources are wasted in this way.

Let us roll the clock forward eighteen months. Mrs G has had her hip replacement and was discharged after twelve days in hospital. She made a good recovery but was still using a stick when she slipped outside her back door and fractured her femur. In hospital she contracted an infection and had to stay in for several weeks. She has lost all confidence as a result of her fall. While in hospital she has shown some signs of vagueness and confusion. Her married daughter who lives 250 miles away visited her in hospital but has discussed with the nursing sister her worries about how her mother will cope on discharge. The sister refers Mrs G to the hospital social services department.

What factors would be relevant to the assessment in this case? There is now more than a single agency involved, and more than a single service request. A simple assessment has become more complex and a different approach is required. This will need to look at a range of factors affecting Mrs G and her ability to live safely at home. These will include:

- The safety of both Mrs G and others
- Her mental health
- Her physical health
- Her ability to cope with activities of daily living

- The social and environmental supports and/or pressures for Mrs G
- The primary carers for Mrs G.

A functional assessment will be required. Given the physical problems which Mrs G has experienced, it would be important to involve an occupational therapist to assess Mrs G's current and anticipated future ability to cope with living again in her own home and in coping with the activities of daily living (ADLs). Much used by the insurance industry as a standard measure of incapacity, ADLs include washing and bathing, toileting, dressing, cooking, cleaning, and shopping.

The OT will be able to advise whether there are any aids or adaptations to property which would help Mrs G to cope at home. But the ability of older people to adapt is very much determined by the social support systems which they have and by their overall psychological attitudes. The OT will be able to assess physical capacity but the care manager needs to investigate social supports.

The first is the degree of help which the family can offer. Mrs G's daughter has a family of her own and is a long way away so is unlikely to be able to offer practical assistance on a regular basis. The care manager will need to explore whether there are other relatives who might be willing to help. The second is the extent of Mrs G's social network and whether neighbours and friends of Mrs G who play a significant part in Mrs G's life might be able to assist either in terms of practical help or as part of a friendship network to address her potential isolation. Depression is something of which the care manager must always be aware. It is important to ensure that a range of contacts is maintained. Introduction to local clubs for older people or in severe cases to local day centres may help to obviate depression. With the suggestion of possible confusion, the care manager needs to be alert to Mrs G's mental condition and simple tests can help to indicate the degree of seriousness.

Risk management

High on the agenda for any care manager is consideration of risk. With the scrutiny to which social services decision-making has been subject, especially in the area of child protection, departments have become risk averse. Similar attention is now being given to the development of inter-agency protocols for adult protection analogous to those which have been in force for twenty years in child protection.

Risk management is a relatively easy business if the task is the elimination of all risk. But in social care a balance has to be struck between the rights of the individual to live as they choose and their right to protection. Is it legitimate for older people to live in squalor with accumulations of old newspapers, rotting food and unkempt animals? Do they have a right to choose or do their neighbours and/or relatives have a right to expect social services to intervene to protect the elderly person . . . even against their will?

Risk management requires an assessment of the degree of incapacity and the risk posed by it across a range of situations including the propensity to social isolation discussed above. These will include:

- risk of falls
- fear of being burgled or mugged

- risk of self-neglect in nutrition – not buying fresh food, storing food too long, not cooking proper meals, etc.
- risk of self-neglect through obliviousness to dirt and mess
- risk of accident posed by confusion – letting kettles boil dry, leaving the gas on, etc.
- risk of hypothermia through inadequate heating or false economies in heating
- risk though admitting strangers in to the house

Listing these considerations has a familiar ring, for few of us have not at some time weighed similar issues in relation to an elderly relative, and whether they can continue to live safely at home. Social workers have become acutely aware of public criticism and their safety-first approach was summed up by a social worker:

> With social work, whether it's with the elderly or with children, the key thing is to cover yourself so that if there is an inquiry of any kind by a relative or a councillor or whoever, you can always say you did the maximum possible within various limitations.
>
> (Davies *et al.* 1990: 183)

Those limitations relate both to the level of resources available and even more powerfully to the legislative framework which governs adult protection. This is still dominated by the compulsory powers in Section 47 of the 1948 National Assistance Act. This gives local authorities the power to remove people from their own homes to a place of safety because they are suffering from grave chronic disease or are physically incapacitated and living in unsanitary conditions. These powers are very rarely used. They require the support of the Director of Public Health and the conditions for compulsory removal are rarely satisfied. They go to the heart of the balancing act between individual and societal rights which is central to the role played by local authorities.

The most recent guidance issued by the Department of Health *No Secrets* (2000a) is unequivocal in its call for the full inter-agency approach which characterizes child protection. This is welcome because in relation to vulnerable adults there is a tendency for agencies to attempt to shunt the responsibility for initiating action elsewhere. Clarity about respective roles, powers and responsibilities should help to address this. The danger, however, is that an organizational structure becomes a substitute for effective action with more attention being paid to compliance with procedures than to the delivery of care. Care managers should use the structures to reinforce their work by ensuring that appropriate cases are identified to the adult protection committee.

The guidance suggests that the concept of 'significant harm' borrowed from the Children Act should be used in adult care covering:

> not only ill treatment (including sexual abuse and forms of ill treatment which are not physical) but also the impairment of, or an avoidable deterioration in, physical or mental health, and the impairment of physical, intellectual, emotional, social or behavioural development.
>
> (Department of Health 2000a: 12)

The guidance is explicit on the implications of the new approach for commissioners.

> Service commissioners, at both national and local level, should ensure that all documents, such as service specifications, invitations to tender and service contracts, fully reflect their policy for the protection of vulnerable adults and specify how they expect providers to meet the requirements of the policy. They should require that any allegation or complaint about abuse that may have occurred within a service subject to contract specifications must be brought to the attention of the contracts officer of any purchasing authority.
>
> (ibid.: 23)

Neighbours are likely to use these guidelines to cover cases of self-neglect where there is a suggestion of failing mental health and physical deterioration. The balance of individual and societal rights will again be tested.

Area of assessment	The source of information, e.g. social worker, home care worker, day centre, carer, community psychiatric nurse, GP, etc. should be identified for each area covered
Background and factual data	Family composition; social history of moves, jobs, key relationships, income, ethnicity, religion, significant life change or loss
Risk and safety issues	Risk of self-neglect, history of domestic accidents, vulnerability to abuse or crime
Health – physical	History of illness/hospitalization; medication; hearing and sight
Health – mental	History of psychological health; attitudes to self and others; risk; depression; confusion; thought disorder; aggression; reaction to life events
Activities of daily living	Personal care; mobility; nutrition; domestic care, e.g. cooking, cleaning; shopping
Communication	Difficulties in communication through speech impairment; deafness; sensory loss; use of sign language; non-verbal communication, etc.
Community links	Relationships with family, friends and neighbours; membership of clubs or community groups; cultural, religious or ethnic affiliations; favoured leisure time pursuits
Accommodation	Owner or tenant; any financial difficulties; garden maintenance; outstanding repairs
Finance	If a service is likely to be offered, more detailed financial information will be necessary on income, outgoings, capital assets, etc.

Figure 4.2 Checklist for care management

The assessment process is one part of care management. Checklists have their place, not as a slavish prescription to be followed in every case, but as an *aide-mémoire* to what has to be covered in a comprehensive assessment. Figure 4.2 is a helpful summary of the ground which needs to be explored.

In this process of assessment each entry should clarify areas where change needs to be effected to improve the quality of life of the individual. This will usually be evident from discussion with the individual or carer. At every stage the views of the client should be noted. A separate section should be completed giving the carer's perspective. This is to be distinguished from the carer's right to ask for a separate assessment which will require the comprehensive approach set out above.

Assessment is the critical part of the community care process. The long list of issues set out above may reinforce that view. There is, however, an important distinction between a systematic approach to a complex task and the mechanistic completion of a checklist. 'The routine collection of standardised data has too often become a substitute for intelligent enquiry' (Middleton 1999). Good assessment is good social work. It needs to be carried out in a way which encourages and involves the user in agreeing the process and timescale for the assessment, in securing the user's views at every stage, and in agreeing with the user and carer objectives where changes are mutually identified as desirable. Many of the skills in building relationships, promoting trust and confidence, and working at a pace determined by the service user are those which have long been core skills in social work practice.

Middleton argues that assessment should be an analytical process by which decisions and plans can be made rather than an exercise in data collection, and sets out the following characteristics of a good assessment:

- Starts with an open mind.
- Starts where the individual is.
- Involves and empowers the user as a partner.
- Relates to their perceived problem and explores the reasons for it.
- Collects only relevant data.
- Puts the information in the context of its collection.
- Analyses the problem using the data.
- Explores the pros and cons of a range of solutions.
- Thinks about a range of options.
- Does not put pressure on the user to choose the option the assessor wants.
- Negotiates with the individual, and with existing service and potential service providers, to find an acceptable and feasible solution.
- Makes recommendations which relate to the information collected.
- Makes arrangements for review.

(Middleton 1994)

Assessing needs

Both the Griffiths Report and the NHS and Community Care Act which gave legislative effect to the proposals reflected the prevailing political philosophy of the time. This believed that too much power was concentrated in the hands of public bodies as monopoly providers of care, with the result that services were overly influenced by the needs of providers rather than users. Day centres for those with mental health problems opened from 9 to 5, closing in the evenings and at weekends when people were at their most vulnerable. Home help hours were organized around the convenience of the root rather than the needs of users. The available services were rationed on a formulaic basis. Users, while accorded respect, were not central to the care process except as recipients.

The guidance on the NHS and Community Care Act made it clear that in future the emphasis was to be on the needs of the service user and how best to meet them instead of requiring users to fit into boxes convenient to the service provider. Flexibility and choice were to be part of this culture change with care managers as the vehicle for delivering the change.

Needs take many forms. They are sometimes desires couched in the language of need. My car is four years old so I might say casually, 'I need to get a new car'. This is a want or desire but certainly not a need. Home care requests sometimes are similar expressions of hope or desire rather than need. Davies and colleagues offer a useful way of differentiating need in terms of the appropriate service response, see Table 4.1.

Table 4.1 Differentiating needs

Independent	Able to maintain acceptable standards of nutrition, cleanliness, warmth and security without help
Long interval needs (the impact will vary according to availability of carer support)	Unable to perform one or more domestic tasks which require to be undertaken occasionally, e.g. difficulty in managing steps, or in shopping
Short interval needs (again, carer support is a key variable)	Unable to perform one or more tasks which have to be undertaken frequently, e.g. preparing meals, bathing
Critical interval needs	Unable to perform regular self-care tasks, e.g. getting out of bed, toileting

Source: Davies *et al.* (1990: 50–1)

In theory, the assessment of needs should lead to an individually tailored care plan. In practice, resource constraints have intervened to make care plans more a statement of the possible than was originally intended. Eligibility criteria – the published and publicly available criteria for services which are publicly funded – set out the basis on which services will be allocated. These criteria govern whether needs are sufficiently acute to meet the threshold for services.

Using the example of Mrs G again, she may like the idea of going to a local day centre for older people to help her to regain her confidence. She would not, however, be certain to get a place. Whether she was eligible would depend on how many places were available locally and the degree to which services were targeted at those most at risk of going into residential care. If there was only one centre in the locality, priority would be given to those otherwise housebound or possibly those with severe dementia – in order to offer a break for the carer. In such circumstances Mrs G could lose out. If, however, there were several centres available, her relatively low level of need – the long interval need of the typology – would secure her a place. Eligibility criteria have become the rationing device used to balance needs against resources.

Despite the scale of the transfer of the Special Transitional Grant, adding over 20 per cent in real terms to social services budgets between 1993 and 1999, there have been severe financial restrictions in many social services authorities. The publicity attached to community care and the emphasis placed on improved information and publicity have led to heightened expectations about what help can be given through social services and increased demand for that provision. Rationing techniques have been used to damp that demand both through eligibility criteria and through increased charges. The hopes in the Griffiths Report for a truly needs-led service have therefore foundered on the reality of resources.

Care planning

The care plan is the instrument setting out the package of care identified by the care manager as best meeting the needs of the individual. It is a written document shared with the service user and their carer, identifying unmet need and desires as well as those needs for which provision has been made. There is no standard national format but some elements are common to all care plans.

Despite the difficult financial context, care plans are the opportunity for creative thinking about responses to the user's situation. Rummery and Glendinning note that the original vision of individualized service provision has been compromised by the financial pressures:

> Assessments have increasingly been used as a mechanism for prioritising needs and restricting access to services for all but those deemed most at risk. Indeed, many social service departments now ration access to assessment itself, through a range of managerial and bureaucratic procedures which effectively delay or circumvent the assessment and care management process for all but those considered to be at the greatest risk of harm.
>
> (2000: 51)

The task of care planning will usually fall to the worker who carried out the assessment. It is, however, a separate process although inevitably some of the options will have been discussed between the worker and the user in the process of developing the assessment. The options need to be wider than the range of services available from the public or independent sectors, for example, linking a housebound individual with mobile library services or the joys and frustrations of Internet shopping could equally be part of a care plan.

The plan should relate to the needs identified in the assessment process. They should be clear in setting out what the objectives are for a specific initiative. If an elderly person is being linked to a day centre, the rationale and objectives should be specified. An example of this would be:

Mrs B is being referred to Glebe House day centre because she is isolated and had a very limited range of social contacts. The aim is to secure her attendance on two days a week to link with her preferred activities – bridge and tai chi. The evaluation of the plan will focus on (a) whether her range of social contacts has been extended; (b) whether her depression is less acute; and (c) any changes in physical and mental agility.

ACTIVITY 4.1: PREPARING A CARE PLAN

Prepare a care plan for Mr and Mrs A, aged 86 and 82 respectively. Mr and Mrs A live in a bungalow which they own. There is no mortgage. They have one married daughter who lives nearly 200 miles away who visits three or four times a year.

Mr A had a heart attack three years ago but made a good recovery and with tablets his condition is under control. Mrs A has Alzheimer's disease and her condition has progressively worsened over the past two years. She wanders particularly at night. Mr A adamantly refuses any idea of residential or respite care, seeing it as his duty to care for his wife. He is, however, finding it increasingly difficult to monitor his wife at night and to cope with her unprompted aggressive outbursts.

The GP is anxious about the impact on Mr A's health. Their daughter reluctantly thinks her mum should go into a home. Neighbours have expressed concern about Mrs A's shouting and bizarre behaviour.

In preparing the plan, outline what you would be aiming to achieve, how would you set about it, and how you would measure the effectiveness of your intervention in 6 months' time.

Implementation of evaluation and monitoring

Writing a care plan and securing the agreement of the client and primary carer to the plan are one thing. Putting it in place is another. There are a number of potential pitfalls. It is difficult to generalize as no two care plans should be identical. In practice, the limited range of choices available to service users and care managers means that there are usually some common areas of difficulty.

First, the plan may involve referral to and use of a service provided not by the local authority but by a third party, usually from the independent sector. The initial contact is critical. If the care manager has established a warm and trusting relationship with the client, that style needs to be carried though in the contact with the provider agency. Any hint of resistance or reservation will be quickly spotted by the client.

Second, the choice will be more limited than the client may have expected at the time of the care plan. Access to services is *de facto* rationed and the choice of care may not be available as anticipated by the user.

Third, despite the emphasis on the multi-skilled worker to cover a range of domestic tasks identified in the PSSRU studies, in practice, demarcation lines continue to exist between different services and different agencies. The client may find more people coming across the threshold than had been anticipated.

In implementing the care plan, the worker needs constantly to check back with the user that the objectives set in the plan remain valid and are being achieved. Plans are not set in stone and may need to be modified in the light of experience. While a pre-planned date for review is necessary, monitoring is a continuous process, not a one-off exercise.

Monitoring

The monitoring of care plans is central to the development of needs-led approaches to service delivery. Needs change and the care plan must be adjusted to reflect those changing needs. Where there are major life changes, for example, a period of hospitalization or bereavement, a full reassessment may be required.

A formal review should be held at least once every six months to consider the validity of the current care plan. That review should be more than a paper exercise and should include the care manager, the home care worker and/or day care worker who works with the client (if applicable), and any primary health care staff involved with the client, and any other key figures. The user and their primary carer should always be fully involved in the review process. The GP's views should be sought although requesting GP attendance at case conferences and reviews is a triumph of hope over experience!

When resources are scarce, it is essential to ensure that they go to those who need them most. The continuing relevance of any service provided needs to be reviewed so that it can be reallocated elsewhere if it is no longer effective.

Evaluation

The process of evaluation follows on naturally from monitoring. It may be formalized in a review process or may take place at the same time as monitoring. The questions to be answered in the evaluation are:

- Does the care plan still meet the needs of the service user or does it need to be amended?
- Are there new needs not reflected in the current care plan?
- Have there been changes in the social support systems available for the service user?
- Have there been changes in the coping capacities of the service user?
- Could the care package be better organized and delivered?

In tracing the seven elements of the care plan, it will be evident that there is some considerable overlap. The elements follow logically but can where appropriate be dealt with at the same time. What is important is that all the stages are covered in the course of the care management process.

WHO ARE THE CARE MANAGERS?

The intention of the Griffiths Report was that care managers would be managerially located in the lead agency – social services – for the delivery of care. The Report, however, was clear that these staff could come from any of the professional disciplines engaged in health and welfare, or none. It was certainly not expected that social work would be the dominant professional background.

This approach reflected some of the findings of the Kent studies. The initial scheme in Kent had involved social workers acting as care managers with a devolved budget.

In subsequent variations of the scheme in Gateshead and Darlington, nurses were employed as care managers as well as social workers to secure the full engagement of primary health care with medical and paramedical staff also serving as part of a multi-disciplinary team. A further variation in Darlington meant that service managers controlled the budget but were able to deploy a team of home care workers. The idea of a multi-skilled primary care worker spanning the roles of home care and nursing auxiliary worker emerged from these studies.

The studies showed two features as critical success factors. First, the devolution of control over resources to the care manager. Without that direct control and authority, it was difficult for care managers to get the priority needed for their client and deliver services which were flexible enough to accommodate individual needs. The second was a difference in the effectiveness of 'administrative' and clinical care management approaches. Administrative models focused on the organizational task of assembling the care package from a menu of possible options. Clinical models included more direct work with the service user to establish their needs. The PSSRU studies confirmed that allocating resources was not an administrative task. Building relationships both with the service user and carer but also with the other staff and workers involved in delivering care was an essential part of the process (Challis *et al.* 1993: 201).

Although the expectation had been that care managers would come from a range of disciplines, in practice, social work has become the usual professional background for those appointed as care managers. In large measure this is because community nursing staff whose skills and experience would have fitted them for the role were very reluctant to move into local authority employment from the NHS. Issues of employment continued to dog potential joint employment and ready transferability until the 1999 Health Act brought in more flexible practices.

The dominant role taken by those already in local authority employment coupled with limitations on resources meant that the transition to the mixed economy with care managers in the vanguard of change has taken a long while to come about. In 1994 Wistow *et al.* identified a number of reasons for the slow pace of development including:

- Financial pressures within social services departments.
- Underdevelopment of alternative suppliers.
- Inadequate technology/systems.
- Unwillingness to consider some alternative providers.
- Political/policy uncertainty.
- Mistrust of the private sector.
- Paucity of alternative suppliers.
- Paucity of volunteers.
- Voluntary agencies unwilling to develop as providers.

(Wistow *et al.* 1994)

It has been commissioning rather than care management which has been the primary driver of change. Care managers have often responded to the political context within which commissioning takes place with imaginative examples of micro-commissioning to improve the range of options available for users. The reality, however, is that many care plans have turned out to be less creative and imaginative than the early advocates of care management would have wished. To the list above one might now add the complications of purchasing across the health and social care divide despite the new opportunities given by the Health Act.

MULTI-DISCIPLINARY APPROACHES TO CARE MANAGEMENT

Intriguingly, in view of the nursing profession's historic lack of interest in care management, the NHS Plan proposes a new role for nurses in coordinating the care of older people following their discharge from hospital. Whether this would be a care management role or something different is not yet clear. The scope for overlap with the current care management role in hospital discharge is evident. It illustrates the influence of political considerations in the sensitive area of acute bed usage.

The opportunities for joint working will make it possible to build on some of the experimental models of care management which have been explored in recent years. Given the development of primary care trusts, those models of joint working with clear links with primary care are of particular interest. Rummery and Glendinning (2000) studied a number of examples of partnership working. Early initiatives prior to the Health Act included the following projects.

Bromsgrove total purchasing project

In this project care managers for older people were employed in a health centre with respite care facilities. The joint-funded team of care managers developed a respite care service and improved access to both domiciliary care and residential care for practice staff. There were major benefits in improved relationships and understanding between primary care staff and social services but detailed work was needed to overcome historic mistrust between the two.

Malmesbury integrated community care team

An integrated primary care and social services team based in a GP practice with occupational therapists, community nurses and social services staff all performing community care assessments. All were able to purchase both health and social care services for patients.

Again, a sustained period of team building was required to deal with the mistrust and suspicion between the occupational groups despite the excellent working relationships which preceded the project. The benefits came in better access to services for patients, improved understanding, and reduced delays in undertaking assessments. There were, however, no measurable differences in service outcome for users or carers.

Care management in a GP practice in Greenwich

Three care managers were based in an urban GP practice. They received referrals from other practice-based staff, and directly from patients. There were many positives including more holistic assessments carried out by the care managers, improved response times and throughput, improved interprofessional communication and enhanced patient satisfaction with what was seen as a diminution of the bureaucracy.

It was not all good news, however. The care managers were seen by both patients and primary care professionals as part of an enhanced NHS. Some primary care professionals were unhelpful in accommodating the care managers who were obliged to fit in with others rather than participating in mutual adjustment. These findings were echoed in a co-location of social workers in an urban practice in Derby.

Derby GP attachment

One and a half full-time equivalent social workers were assigned to cover five urban GP practices with referrals coming from other primary care professionals and direct from patients and families. These social workers did not directly undertake care management functions which remained in the district team.

The benefits from the project were as in other initiatives improved access, responsiveness and mutual understanding. Patients enjoyed quicker access without the sense of stigma which still attaches itself to social services. There was better feedback to primary care staff following referrals.

There were, however, problems. The location of continuing responsibility for care management in the district team meant that the attached social workers spent a disproportionate amount of their time on welfare benefits and housing issues. There was a lack of clarity about their role and the social workers carried high workloads with little support. There was no evidence of better or more speedy multi-disciplinary assessments.

Reviewing this evidence, Rummery and Glendinning conclude that there is clear evidence of benefits in mutual understanding and improved access to patients both in terms of speed of access and reduced bureaucracy from the attachments. However, they conclude that:

- The commitment of key managers and budget holders in both organizations is necessary for sustainable collaboration.
- Collaboration needs to have benefits for both sides involved; the costs should not be borne unequally by one side.
- Participants need to have realistic achievable goals.
- The roles and responsibilities of participants need to be clearly understood at the outset.
- It is particularly important to ensure that community nurses are fully involved.
- The barriers to inter-organizational and inter-professional collaboration should be fully acknowledged.

(Rummery and Glendinning 2000: 78)

It is that last point which is so striking about each of the projects reviewed. Co-location may be a necessary condition for improved partnership working but is not sufficient in itself. There are many obstacles and clarity about who does what is essential if difficulties are to be avoided. Encouragingly, however, those who most appreciated the change were the patients who experienced a less complex and bureaucratic structure.

KEY POINTS

☐   Care management is central to the delivery of the NHS and Community Care Act.

☐   Assessment is the dominant role within care management.

☐   A comprehensive assessment requires detailed knowledge of the user and their needs.

☐   Risk management is an important function of care planning.

☐   Multi-disciplinary care management has many advantages but some problems in implementation.

KEY READING

The Personal Social Services Research Unit dominates the literature. Its detail and statistical tables mean that its work is not always the most accessible to the non-academic reader. *Resources, Needs and Outcomes in Community-based Care* (1990) by Davies, Bebbington and Charnley is a characteristically thorough analysis. An interesting international perspective is provided by another PSSRU publication by Davies, *Care Management, Equity and Efficiency* (1992). More practical help is available in Seed and Kaye's *Handbook for Assessing and Managing Care in the Community* (1994). Baldwin, in *Care Management and Community Care* (2000) offers interesting insights into the way in which practitioner discretion is used in care management. Ways in which the resources of the community can be brought into play are the theme of *Networking and Community Partnership* (1999) by Trevellion.

CHAPTER 5

CONTRACTING

OBJECTIVES

By the end of this chapter you should be able to:

■ Understand the different types of contract used in social care.

■ Be aware of some of the potential pitfalls in the contract process.

■ Know when to involve lawyers and when to ignore them.

■ Minimize the risks to the organization in contracting.

WHEN DO YOU NEED A CONTRACT?

The development of contracting in social care is the lasting legacy of the market economy. Chapter 1 identified the way in which concepts derived from the market came to influence the development of social services departments and social care. That trend is still continuing with a retreat from direct provision of public services by workers employed in the public sector. Instead the role of social services is now seen as one of securing good quality care and ensuring that it is delivered. Effective commissioning is the route to the former and contracting is seen as the vehicle to deliver quality services.

　　Understanding how contracts work, the different types of contract, the enforceability of contracts and ways in which contracts can be made to work for you is an essential part of the overall commissioning task.

What is a contract?

A contract is an agreement between two parties, usually but not always written, under which one party undertakes to carry out a service in exchange for a consideration, usually payment but possibly another service or a transfer of assets as in a barter agreement. It is legally binding and can be enforced through the courts if one party is in default of the contract.

A contract is helpful in ensuring that the promised service is carried out to the agreed specification. It clarifies issues of payment, and establishes the mutual expectations of both parties. Without a contract relationships can become fraught and misunderstandings legion. Courts will sometimes imply a contract even if there is no written documentation.

Before considering the different types of contract and the circumstances in which one might be preferable to another, it is important to go back to first principles. This is essential in major contracts involving building work but can be useful in other situations.

KNOWING WHAT YOU WANT

The first principle can be summed up in one word – WHY? Why is this service needed? Have other options been considered? Have all parties been involved in coming to this conclusion about the service?

Sometimes this is a formal options appraisal process listing out the possibilities including the status quo and setting down formally the pros and cons of each option. A variety of techniques can be used to help to structure decision-making in complex situations.

The largest contracts in which social care is likely to be directly involved are building contracts for a new home or day centre where costs can run into several million pounds. Yet thinking about residential care is shifting rapidly. It is not just whether the development should be left to the private sector or whether innovative forms of partnership through the Private Finance Initiative (PFI) can be brought into play. It is whether there is a continuing role for the traditional residential home or whether other models like intensively supported housing may be more effective. Is there scope for partnership working with health in developing intermediate care? Is dementia best dealt with separately? All these issues need to be addressed well in advance of going out to tender as in building contracts it is not possible to change direction halfway through the project. Ideally they should be resolved before the brief is prepared. That is the task of the Project Team.

What is the role of the Project Team?

The Project Team is the key group which should include the manager responsible for the service, staff with specialist expertise in contracting and finance, staff with experience of the project under consideration (for example, if it is a project for a day centre, the team should have a day centre manager). Design expertise can be added at a later stage but the first task is to establish the needs of the service against the type of issues set out above.

Getting a clear brief for the scheme – whether it is a building project or a major service development – is essential. That requires the project team to thrash out exactly what type of provision it wants, for whom it wants it and when it wants it. Putting this down on paper is a good discipline in resolving at an early stage some of the key issues. The brief can be widely circulated and tested to ensure a wide measure of support for the scheme proposals.

All major building projects have a long lead time. There are severe limitations on the availability of capital finance. This creates a real danger that when money becomes available, possibly through a special credit approval or capital receipts or a partnership deal with the private sector, projects speed ahead without reconsidering whether circumstances have changed.

One way in which this can be addressed is value management (VM), a technique commended by the Audit Commission's study on capital programme management. Value management is a technique

> [to] raise fundamental questions such as: Do we need to build at all? Do we have to build as much? Can we meet needs differently? . . . VM is characterised by workshop meetings, involving the client and the design team, that are held at key stages of the project and are led by an experienced facilitator.
>
> (Audit Commission 1996)

The workshops need to include all the key players. If there is a health care element to the scheme, it is vital to ensure representation from health colleagues and that should be at an appropriate level for decisions. If there are potential legal issues – restrictive covenants – or planning considerations, representatives from those services need to be included. Essentially, VM workshops are the application of a whole systems approach to capital projects in the inception stage. The hothouse atmosphere of a properly prepared day enables a great deal of ground to be covered in a short time and can serve to reinforce the collective ownership of the scheme.

An important element in the process is the identification and weighting of risks to the project. What might go wrong? Political opposition, overspending elsewhere in the capital programme, opposition from local residents, cost overruns on the project, changes in key personnel, insolvency of the contractor can all be considered and weighted for importance with robust contingency plans being developed for those risks regarded as the greatest.

This process helps the project team to be confident in moving forward that all options have properly been explored. The team can then revise the service brief and develop a statement of the operational requirements for the project. This will cover the objectives of the service, how it will be delivered, staffing and service issues, the budget and monitoring arrangements. Most of this task will be the responsibility of the service manager but the team needs to share responsibility and fully understand the issues.

One early issue is the procurement process to be followed. The contract specialist will advise whether the contract is of a scale likely to fall within European Union Contract Regulations and thus require advertisement in the European Journal. This will add significantly to the timescale of tendering, but applies to all contracts in excess of the threshold (set in euros and approximately £3.9 million pounds for building works but only £144,000 for service contracts at the time of writing, May 2001). If the contract is for services over a four-year period, the total payable is aggregated so even relatively small-scale contracts can be caught under these regulations. The regulations differ for different types of contract so this is one area in which it is essential to seek advice from specialist staff.

Different types of contract in social care

There are three main types of contract in use in social care – block contracts, spot contracts, and cost and volume contracts. It is important clearly to understand the differences and the circumstances in which each may be appropriate.

Block contracts

These contracts are for the provision of a given service. This could be the supply of meals on wheels, places in a residential care home or the provision of cleaning services from a firm of contract cleaners. Local authorities like block contracts because:

- They simplify administration.
- They result in lower unit costs and better value for money.
- They provide more stability and continuity for providers.
- They create greater certainty over the supply of the service and referral arrangements.
- They provide the basis for strategic partnering between the local authority and a number of service providers.
- They lead to continuous improvement of services through local authorities having a more substantial stake in the services and providers having more stability.

This list of advantages of block contracts is taken from guidance issued by the Department of the Environment Transport and the Regions called *Supporting People* (2000). It deserves closer examination:

- *Simplicity*: block contracts are easier to manage. The service, the payment and the performance monitoring arrangements are agreed in advance. There are no complicating factors like variable levels of payment or individualized service plans. They are the type of contract with which local authorities are familiar in contexts other than social care.

- *Lower unit costs and better value for money*: this is less obvious in the context of social care. Other forms of contract may deliver better value for money because they are better tailored to individual needs. Volume of service is not the only issue. Direct payments by the service user were a response to the inflexibility and lack of control experienced by users. If the block contractor offers a lower cost but an ineffective service, there is certainly not better value. One has to cost in the time and resource spent in dealing with complaints!

- *Stability and continuity*: definitely a plus point for block contracts. They are for an extended period, often several years, which helps both the commissioner and the provider to plan with confidence. They can also give time for the confidence of the user in the provider to be built up so that the provider secures the type of loyalty which the public sector has often enjoyed as a provider.

- *Certainty about supply and referral arrangements*: this is less obviously true. Referral arrangements are central to the delivery of social care because recipients of the service have to meet the eligibility criteria. The basis of referrals will be common whatever the form of contract. Large contractors with the security of a block contract may be better placed to deliver certainty about supply because they have access to alternatives if a meals on wheels van breaks down or a boiler system collapses.

- *Strategic partnering*: the concept of partnering is a relatively new development in social care. Block contracts in the past tended to be characterized like building contracts by a potentially adversarial relationship in which both parties were seeking competitive advantage from the contract. The Audit Commission study of local authority contracting (1997) referred to the way in which some commercial organizations had developed partnerships with their suppliers which created a win-win position in which suppliers had greater long-term security but worked with the purchaser on the generation of cost savings. Partnering is now also being applied in construction contracts.

    An example of this is the agreement reached between Surrey County Council and Anchor Trust on the transfer of homes and upgrading of standards in which the two parties had worked together and continued to work together after the transfer in a long-term arrangement.

- *Continuous improvement*: this is really an extension of the point about partnership. Building on the long-term nature of the relationship may encourage the search for continuous improvement both in cost and quality. Again, however, long-term relationships are not necessarily synonymous with block contacts. Cost and volume contracts or even spot purchasing from a preferred provider list may give the purchasing authority sufficient leverage to deliver the continuous improvement sought.

Spot contracts

Spot contracts are the basis for individual units of service. A single residential placement in a geographical location to meet the statutory direction on choice might be a specific spot contract. An agreement with a local voluntary organization to extend their normal day service to provide one-to-one supervision for a particular disabled user could be a spot contract. It is specific to the situation and usually negotiated swiftly because there is no time for the normal contracting procedures to be undertaken.

    The advantages to personal social services of spot contracting are evident. These include:

- They are designed to meet a specific set of circumstances and needs personal to the individual.
- They avoid the one-size-fits-all approach of block contracts and are far more flexible.

- They can be established relatively quickly because the basis of the contract is a specific situation. Unlike block contracts one does not have to anticipate every possible contingency in the contract conditions.
- Performance monitoring criteria are more easily established because they can be derived from the satisfaction of the user with the service delivered.

Disadvantages: there is a price to be paid for flexibility both in cost and in resources. The liabilities include:

- The cost of multiple contract arrangements are high in staff time in negotiating with different providers.
- Consistency of approach is more difficult to achieve.
- Contract monitoring is difficult because of the variety of contract arrangements a large county could have up to 500 residential and nursing home placements a year. Monitoring 500 separate contracts would be very time-consuming.

Cost and volume contracts

These are contracts where the agreement is to purchase services at an agreed price but the price may vary according to the volume of service bought. For example, a local authority contracts with a local high quality private provider for residential care places. It could block contract for thirty places at £360 per week or spot contract for each individual at a quoted price of £405 per week. Instead it contracts on the basis of usage, saying it will pay £400 per week for the first 10 placements a year, £380 per week if it places between 10 and 15 a year, £370 if it places 15–20 and £365 if it places more than 20 a year.

Advantages: these contracts are useful because:

- they manage unpredictability in service volume where the level of demand is uncertain
- they guarantee a fixed level of costs
- they give flexibility over an extended time period

Disadvantages: the downside of such contracts relates to best value:

- the cost per placement is higher than under a block arrangement
- the level of pre-contract negotiation is similar to a block contract
- the variable pricing element creates additional accounting costs
- there may be an incentive to place regardless of need to secure a lower unit price

One variant of the cost and volume contract is the call-off contract. Here a provider agrees to provide a service for a fixed fee regardless of volume and in effect is available on a stand-by basis to be used as and when required. It is usually linked with an approved provider list so that the authority can be satisfied about basic quality standards.

PREFERRED PROVIDER LISTS

With spot purchasing the authority has contract arrangements with a wide range of providers. It could have contracts with residential homes in many different parts of the country as users choose to be near their roots, or close to family contacts.

In order better to manage this complexity and to handle call-off contracts, some authorities have established preferred provider lists. This enables prospective providers to apply and be placed on a list so that placements can be made without a further necessity for checking procedures. Providers have to demonstrate that they meet the quality criteria of the authority before they are placed on the list. Procedures vary but will usually include at least one visit by the agency to the provider to ensure that the information offered is accurate.

This can be advantageous to both the purchaser and provider. The advantages of this procedure are:

- Time: the list of potential providers is clearly defined before the process begins with consequent savings on preliminaries and on multiple documentation.
- Closer working relationships between purchasers and providers.
- Shared knowledge about price, quality and user views. Instead of relying only on user survey feedback, the information gap between purchaser and provider can be bridged.
- Mutual trust: the preferred provider is less likely to try to pad a contract price because the stakes are higher and there is a clear mutuality of interest.

There are, however, some problems with preferred provider lists and these need to be recognized. These include the following:

- The barriers erected against new providers. Some local authorities require evidence of past performance, three years trading accounts, £5 million public liability insurance cover, and similar requirements which militate against a new provider.
- Less likelihood of innovative solutions as the preferred providers are more likely to have well-established approaches.
- Less diversity in individual care packages as care managers have their room for manoeuvre circumscribed.

Knapp and Forder concluded a review of preferred provider lists:

> a preferred provider list may be more appropriate: where there are potentially heavy informational imperfections; when local authority market power – while delivering price concessions and high standards – will not destroy providers' desirable or traditional characteristics; and when there is scope for economies of scale in negotiations, specification of contracts and monitoring.
>
> (Knapp and Forder 1993)

The purchaser can make placements more speedily because they know that a given standard of care is on offer and the price for that care. The provider knows the standards which have to be met and has expectations of some business being placed. Neither party, however, knows the likely volume of business because it is dependent on individual preferences.

Such lists are also used for the provision of agency staff – a growth business in local authorities as staff shortages are acute in some areas. With the proliferation of staffing agencies, each with slightly different terms and conditions, the establishment of an approved list enables the authority to set its standards and secure agency compliance. Many authorities also use this to get a differentiated picture to avoid over-dependence on any one agency. Thus it might use Agencies A, B and C for residential staff, C, D and F for fieldwork staff, and B, E and G for domiciliary care staff. In this way it can derive maximum benefit from any specialist expertise without being too tied to a single provider.

But given that every form of contract has disadvantages as well as its positive points, how does one decide what form of contract to use and how can one best safeguard the interests of the purchaser?

ACTIVITY 5.1: DESKTOP EXERCISE

Quick examples may help to clarify this point. Imagine that you are the lead commissioner for adult services. On your desk this morning are three issues.

- The council has decided to externalize all its catering in residential homes. The Chair of Social Services was told by a fellow chair in a neighbouring authority that there are big savings to be made this way.
- A social worker has written a detailed history of a severely disabled woman with a progressive illness who needs specialist care. The social worker proposes a care package comprising night sitting by a local voluntary organization, specialist day care in a unit 10 miles away but in the neighbouring authority, and domiciliary care by the existing care provider.
- You have received a complaint from a Muslim organization about the failure of the meals on wheels service to provide meals using Halal meat. The council is committed to equal opportunity and ethnic-sensitive services and is anxious to respond positively.

What approach to contracting would you take in each of these circumstances? Are there other options and what would be the consequences?

TENDER DOCUMENTATION AND SELECTION

The importance of accurate information about the specification of the service is a recurrent theme of this book. That detail should be reflected in the operational requirement and service brief. Its accuracy is crucial to the success of the contracting process. Tenderers will quote prices on the basis of what they are asked to deliver, not what they think would be the best possible service. Any subsequent variation or enhancement of the brief will carry a cost for the commissioning authority.

Social care is a very different business to construction. It is fast changing in terms of standards and approaches. Yet in contracts the tender document has to be the moment when the service requirements are crystallized and then no longer subject to significant change. That discipline has to be held throughout the organization if major cost over-runs are to be avoided on contracts.

Although there is a technical element in the preparation of tender documents, the service manager has to be responsible for the process and carry the responsibility for signing it off before the organization goes out to tender.

Tendering

After the invitation to tender and the despatch of tender documentation, there is an interim period in which tenders are being prepared. During this period it is essential to have control over the contact between the authority seeking tenders and potential contractors. This can best be achieved by agreeing that only one person is authorized to deal with queries and that person should be a contract specialist.

There are three reasons for this. First, it ensures that the information supplied to any contractor is available to all. Second it ensures that the information is given out consistently both in content and in the degree of detail. Finally, it acts as a safeguard against potential corruption by establishing clear lines of accountability. This may sound over-sensitive to those unfamiliar with contracts but all these processes are open to challenge.

CASE STUDY 10: FAIRNESS TO ALL

A contract is being let for a community support scheme for people with mental health problems. There are two potential bidders – a local voluntary user-led organization and a private company active in delivering community support services to other care groups. The private company knows staff in the local authority and finds out that the costs of providing the service at present are £108,000. It also establishes that the uncertainty about the future of the service means that it is currently staffed wholly by agency staff. The voluntary group advised by the local Council for Voluntary Service submits a tender based on either meeting redundancy costs or applying the same terms and conditions to transferring staff. The private bidder can submit a lower tender because it knows these costs will not arise. It has secured a competitive advantage because it has information not available to the other party.

Fairness in tendering is about equal treatment for all contractors.

Selection procedures

The concept of fairness also has to be applied in selection. Local authorities have strict rules governing the return of tenders with strict deadlines which are rigorously enforced.

The haste to meet the deadline means that sometimes arithmetical errors creep into tender documents so an initial check needs to be made of the accuracy of the returns. Where there has been an error, tenderers have to be asked to clarify the figure returned. Where there has been a major miscalculation, tenderers may opt to withdraw.

Selection does not have to be restricted to the written submission although again this needs to be made clear to prospective tenderers. It is often helpful to include a presentation as a part of the selection. This gives an opportunity to see how fully the tenderer has understood the brief and their sensitivity to any special service requirements. Practicality dictates that only a limited number of presentations can be seen, so a preliminary sift of tenders against the pre-agreed selection criteria may be necessary.

The criteria for selection will vary somewhat according to the nature of the contract. If it is a personal care service, experience may have a higher weighting than financial standing. For a major building contract the financial stability of the contractor will be a major consideration while the level of qualifications of the staff employed a lesser one. Some criteria are, however, likely to be common. These will include:

- previous experience
- track record in similar work including references
- skill and knowledge of the service area
- quality of service set out in tender
- calibre of staff employed
- price
- financial standing and stability

Each requires some qualification. This is not a matter of ticking the relevant box – judgement has to be used by the selection panel – first in weighting the selection criteria for the nature of the contract, and, second, in ranking the tenderers against each criteria to get an overall rank order.

Previous experience in work of a similar nature will always be more relevant than general work in social care. References attract a generally cynical response but can be important in demonstrating that the contractor has delivered successfully elsewhere. As in recruitment it is always useful to make a phone call to ensure that the written reference gives a rounded picture of the contractors' performance.

Price is always a vital factor but Chapter 6 sets out some cautions about looking only at the headline figure in any tender. The approach taken by the tenderer may have cost implications for the commissioning agency, for example, in relation to redundancy or the write-off of capital equipment. One way of dealing with over-emphasis on price as the determining criterion is to look at the quality issues first and assess the tenders against those criteria before considering price.

The criteria, the weightings and the recommendation need to be formally recorded. Often a committee report may be required but even where it is not, the basis for the decision should be clear. Again, this is a protection against any subsequent disputes.

Between selection and contract

There is a temptation after the detailed work leading to the tender and selection process to assume that the task is virtually done. The unhappy experience of the Dome where after the sale of the building was agreed the bidder withdrew shortly before signing the contract is a reminder that things can still go awry after the handshakes and smiles of the initial agreement with the successful contractor. The post-selection discussions are an important part of the process of cementing the relationship between the contractor and the commissioner.

Where there has been a competitive bidding process the successful bidder will be anxious that they may have offered too much if they are buying, or under-priced their service if they are selling. They will want reassurance that the margin they anticipated on the contract can actually be achieved. Sometimes they may seek to vary provisions as set out in the original tender documentation. These variations may be minor – changing the basis for billing – or they may go to the heart of the contract.

It is therefore again important to ensure that the accountability line for decisions is clearly established. The service manager will be best placed to do this as they will be involved in discussions about the handover arrangements, the start date for the contract and the monitoring mechanisms which will be used.

CONTRACT CONDITIONS

Contracts are legal documents. They contain conditions designed to cover all contingencies and to protect the interests of the person letting the contract. But in addition to the standard conditions of contract covering issues such as confidentiality, corrupt gifts and payments, timetabling, default mechanisms, health and safety and enforcement notices, some public authorities have included conditions designed to promote specific issues.

A standard clause on discrimination in government contracts reads:

> Neither party shall unlawfully discriminate either directly or indirectly on such grounds as gender, race, colour, ethnic or national origin, within the meaning of the Sex Discrimination Act 1975, the Race Relations Act 1976 or the Disabilities Discrimination Act 1995.
>
> In the course of performing this contract both parties shall give all due regard to the provisions of the Human Rights Act 1998 and to comply with their respective obligations as they may apply to this Contract.

This clause is a modest clause requiring compliance with the law. Some authorities include in their standard conditions clauses which positively promote equality of opportunity. Examples include clauses requiring the use of a proportion of local staff in the workforce, clauses which require contractors to have a written equal opportunities policy and to monitor the composition of their workforce, and clauses which give sexual orientation the same legal protection afforded by race relations and sex discrimination legislation.

The basis for such clauses will be familiar and welcome in social care where staff are often genuinely committed to anti-discriminatory practice. They are acutely aware of the degree of institutional racism. It is salutary to carry out a simple check if you believe that your organization is free of the taint of institutional racism. How many staff were dismissed in the last twelve months? How many of these were black or Asian? Is this higher or lower than the proportion of black or Asian staff in the workplace?

There has, however, to be a caution about the inclusion of clauses which are unenforceable. Pay rates in social care jobs are low and preference to local labour may be difficult to achieve if there is a local factory offering better rates of pay. Monitoring of the composition of the workforce is a legitimate requirement. Requiring the contractor to ensure that his workforce was better balanced with more black and Asian staff in managerial positions would, however, be viewed as beyond the lawful scope of the contract. Getting legal advice is imperative in this difficult and sensitive area.

MONITORING CONTRACTS

The contractor will be subject to monitoring procedures as set out in the contract. These will usually include:

- regular flows of financial and service information
- performance standards set in the contract covering both volume and quality issues
- staffing levels

The contract will usually be specific on the use to which this data will be put. It is good practice to have a regular meeting between the service manager and the contractor to review how the contract is going. Such meetings should be at least quarterly and in the case of large contracts could be monthly. The data which has been supplied could be discussed together with any problems arising for either party from the contract.

Examples of the type of issues which can usefully be discussed in this forum include complaints, changes in workload, good practice developments identified by Audit Commission or Social Services Inspectorate reviews of similar services and anything likely to have an impact on pricing at a later stage.

These regular meetings need to be differentiated from a formal contract review meeting which should be held at least once a year where all aspects of the contract can be discussed.

DEFAULT

Contracts should have a mechanism for dealing with poor performance on the part of the contractor. The usual procedure would cover enforcement notices, termination and damages.

Enforcement notices

Where there are concerns about the performance of the contractor, these should first be raised in the regular business meeting between the contractor and the service manager. The contractor should be clear about the nature of concern and agree remedial action with the service manager. That forum provides a regular opportunity to review progress in addressing the problems.

Only if no progress is being made or if the situation is worsening would an authority wish to take the serious step of issuing an enforcement notice. These notices are not to be used as a warning shot across the bows. They are the first step towards formal termination and need therefore to be used only if termination is a real option.

The notice has to specify the default in performance and give a period of notice, usually 30 days, within which the default has to be addressed to the satisfaction of the authority. If the failing is not addressed, the authority has the right to terminate the contract immediately.

Termination

The enforcement notice is one situation which can lead to immediate termination. Other such situations are:

- The default is not capable of remedy, for example, a breakdown in service through loss of staff.
- The default is a fundamental breach of the contract. This is a fertile area for case law and best to be avoided through enforcement notice procedures if possible.
- The contractor goes bankrupt.
- The contractor undergoes a change of control with an adverse impact on the performance of the contract.

Termination invariably brings problems in its wake. First, there is the inevitable interruption to the supply of the service. This may be a delay in completing a building or home care clients going unvisited. It has a cost for the authority. Second, termination will often be accompanied by legal action which also carries costs. Finally, there will be costs involved in organizing an interim solution or in re-tendering.

Before enforcement notices are served, it is therefore vital that the authority is clear about its fall-back position and what it intends to do in the event of termination. Preparatory work should start prior to the commencement of the enforcement notice if that is possible without destabilizing the current contractor and undermining their chances of putting matters right.

Damages

While damages may be payable if there has been a failure on the part of the contractor to deliver the agreed service, the cost of recovery may well exceed the amount achieved. First, legal costs will be incurred; second, it will take a long time to reach a court hearing with costs, both real and opportunity, incurred in preparing statements for the court and assembling all the documentation; third, courts are not necessarily sympathetic to a large public authority pursuing a small concern for damages; finally, courts will place a value on the work which was actually undertaken, however inadequate it may have been. If damages are awarded they will be judged on the basis of restoring the status quo before the contract and will not be punitive.

The threat of legal action is one thing. Carrying it through takes time, energy and resources. It will rarely deliver the full sum in satisfaction which your lawyers initially advised you could secure. Proceed with caution is the advice.

The various aspects of contracts have been considered in detail. There are two other aspects which need to be considered as particularly relevant in the context of social care. These are service agreements and contract extensions.

SERVICE AGREEMENTS

Service agreements are binding agreements between two parties but without the formality and legal associations of a full contract. They are used most frequently in relation to small-scale voluntary organizations delivering a service on behalf of a public authority. As the service is usually performed for payment, such agreements are probably contracts in law but their different designation as service agreements means that both parties are tacitly acknowledging that they will not be enforced.

This does not lessen the significance of the agreements. No public body will hand over cash without being clear and specific about the nature of the service to be delivered. This service specification will be matched by specific targets against which the performance of the provider will be judged. The overall performance in turn will influence decisions about the renewal of the service agreement.

ACTIVITY 5.2: CHOOSING THE RIGHT AGREEMENT

A local voluntary organization working with people with mental health problems opens a drop-in café attached to a day centre with a grant from a trust. The funding is for a two-year pilot project. Eighteen months into the scheme the group approaches the local authority to pick up the £35,000 per annum funding. Assuming this was generally felt to be a useful service and funding was available – both potentially big 'ifs' – how would you approach this? Would you seek a contract or a service agreement? What performance standards would you seek to secure from the organization?

As a footnote to this example it is worth noting that dealings with voluntary groups are rarely on the basis of 100 per cent funding. It is likely that the organization will raise some funds through local activity and may have access to trust funding on a minor scale which could offset the initial request for full funding. The brokerage role of local authorities is used as the lead funder but constituting part of a consortium of funding sources. Many trusts will be reassured if the local authority is part funder of a project as this can unlock the door to complementary funding support.

CONTRACT EXTENSIONS

Most contracts are for finite periods. They will, however, contain provision for an extension by mutual consent. This can be for a year or exceptionally for two years but should not be for longer. The circumstances in which a contract extension could be considered are:

- the lack of alternative providers
- a pending reorganization of the service
- doubts about a continuing requirement for the service
- anticipated operational difficulties in re-tendering

Any extension will normally roll over the existing terms and conditions including pricing for a further period. Extensions should not be given as a reward for good performance. There should be a clear justification for extending the life of the contract which will withstand the scrutiny of both elected members and external auditors.

CASE STUDY 11: DECIDING ON EXTENSIONS

A Best Value review of residential care provision for older people is under way. There are three in-house homes and seventeen provided by the independent sector. The local authority spot purchases from eleven and has a block contract for fifteen places with one provider who has the largest home but can offer specialist dementia care. This contract is due to run out next month but the Best Value review has hardly started. It is thought likely that this may recommend the closure or externalization of the in-house provision and greater use of the independent sector. Given these circumstances, would you extend the contract and, if so, what justifications would you propose to members for your recommendation?

A suggested response to this case study is given in Chapter 9.

NOT QUITE 57 VARIETIES

The range of contracting procedures now being adopted in social care is neatly illustrated by the issue of *Community Care* of 5–11 October 2000b. The issue is not unusual and was selected because it was to hand when writing this chapter. Under the heading 'Tenders' there are seven advertisements from local authorities.

Of the seven, two are straightforward requests for tenders for the provision of intensive domiciliary home support and for an independent visitors service, respectively. Full tender documents are available on request and the advertisements ask for nothing more than suitable qualifications and experience at this stage. A third invites expressions of interest in taking over a community alarm service currently provided by social services on the basis of a five-year contract.

The remaining four are more complex and illustrate that various options have been seriously considered. Authority A seeks expressions of interest to provide a Family Centre service, including core assessments in respect of families referred, assessment of parenting capability for care proceedings and court attendance as well as programmes of group and individual work. The council will provide the premises under lease.

Authority B seeks expressions of interest to supply a specialist social care and housing management service in a high care hostel for people with severe mental health problems. The advertisement gives detail about the nature of the unit, of the assured shorthold tenure and the requirement to work with the council and the housing provider to maximize independence of users. A formal tender process will follow the expressions of interest.

Authority C is seeking applications for the supply of domiciliary home care service from suitably qualified and experienced providers. It is awarding block contracts and establishing an approved provider list. It intends both to award block contracts and to spot purchase from those providers on the approved list. The advertisement spells out the size of contracts anticipated as between 500 hours and 2000 hours a week.

Authority D is even more specific. It is seeking expressions of interest for home care services on the basis of two types of contract – block contracts for twelve months with a possible twelve months extension in a defined geographical area, and call-off contracts for a similar period but with no guaranteed minimum volume of work.

The council wants to consult with care providers prior to the issue of tenders but will also use the preliminary period to weed out some providers by 'a financial and technical assessment of care providers by way of questionnaire and interview'. It offers an information evening to explain the council's requirements.

The spirit of partnership is beginning to develop. Flexibility is coming into the process and careful thought is being given to the best form of contract in these examples.

As commissioner and purchaser your task is to see the big picture and ensure that the contract serves the needs of the organization. That means ensuring that the service is specified accurately and described accurately in the tender documentation. That means ensuring that the payment terms meet the demands of Best Value and that the position of the contracting organization is protected if the contractor defaults in the performance of the contract. And it means ensuring that performance standards and monitoring mechanisms are in place to keep the contractor's standards up to the level required.

Contracts are, however, means. They serve the needs of the organization and must not be allowed to dominate. The traditional conflict model of contracting is rarely suitable for social care where both commissioner and contractor bring to the task the same values and commitment. Building effective partnerships may mean cutting through some of the arm's-length approach to building contracting and developing a true sense of a shared endeavour. That, however, has to be set against the requirements of equity which have been stressed above.

One thing is certain. Contracting for social care will increase as in-house provision is reduced. Getting best value from that process is a task to which the organization as a whole has to be committed. Public sector management is subject to increasing scrutiny and good practice in contracting can help to meet that test.

KEY POINTS

☐   There are different types of contract, each with advantages and disadvantages.

☐   Getting the service specification right is a key success factor in contracting.

☐   Selection procedures have to be scrupulously fair.

☐   Caution is necessary before taking legal action to secure enforcement.

☐   Be clear why you are extending the term of the contract.

KEY READING

The two Audit Commission publications *Just Capital* (1996) and *Take your Choice* (1997) are good introductions to best practice in the use of resources and to the role of contracting in securing it. Two workbooks produced soon after the introduction of community care contain helpful exercises – *Contracting in the Community Care Market* (1994) by Flynn and Hurley and *Managing Contracts* (1994) by Lawrie. *Contracts, Cooperation and Competition* (1997) by Deakin and Mackie is more legalistic. A better overall picture of the impact on public services comes from *The Contract Culture in Public Services* (1997) by Perri 6 and Kendall. The best concise treatment of the issues is *Public Sector Management* (1997) by Flynn, especially Chapters 7 and 8.

CHAPTER 6

COSTS AND PRICES

OBJECTIVES

By the end of this chapter you should understand:

■ Direct costs and overheads, and how to establish a unit cost for services.

■ The importance of marginal costs in contracting.

■ Cost effectiveness and how it differs from cost-benefit analysis.

■ The process of analysing tender prices and identifying possible areas for saving.

DIRECT COSTS AND OVERHEADS

The Bourbons were accused of knowing the price of everything and the value of nothing. Social care commissioners have been subject to the same criticism. In the eternal trade-off between price and quality, they have been accused of focusing almost exclusively on price because that is measurable whereas measures of quality are more elusive. Given the pressure to drive down costs, which has been a constant for many years, the focus on costs is unsurprising. But few social care managers understand how costs are made up, the significance of unit costs and marginal costs and how to go about scrutinizing costs whether in a tender or an in-house service.

It costs £350 per week to keep somebody in residential care. That type of unit cost figure is often used in debate and discussion but few have much idea of what goes into that headline weekly cost. It is certainly hard to reconcile with our personal daily living costs and suggests waste and profligacy on the part of providers. The example of Mr Brown's care will illustrate the reality of care costs.

Mr Brown occupies a single room in a residential home. The home is located in a large Edwardian house which has been converted and which incorporates an extension to give thirty places overall. He takes meals in the lounge of a wing serving eight rooms, except for lunch which is served in the communal dining room. Although able to get about with a frame he needs help with bathing and has some continence problems. He takes part in the Bingo sessions twice a week but spends most of his time watching TV or playing cards with two other men in the home.

If Mr Brown was still living in his own home his pension would pay for his food, heating, lighting, electricity, clothes and shopping. In the residential home the same costs have to be covered. Food is even more important in a residential setting than it was when Mr Brown lived at home. When we go away to a hotel or to a foreign country, food is one of the key ways in which we define the quality of the experience. For many years local authorities engaged in the bulk buying of provisions for all their residential homes seeing savings in economies of scale and standardization. Now they have increasingly delegated responsibility for purchasing to the Head of the home. This makes sense both because the Head is best placed to assess residents' likes and dislikes and can also negotiate with local providers and thus contribute in a small way to the local economy. It also gives more opportunity for creativity and inventiveness on the part of the catering staff.

Heating costs charged to Mr Brown are higher than he would have paid in his own home. First, he is now living in an older building with high ceilings which takes more energy to heat; second, the home is kept at a higher average temperature than Mr Brown was used to in order to accommodate the frailty of the residents; third, there is no personal incentive to save on the bills whereas Mr Brown used to heat only the room he was using at the time and turn the heating off elsewhere. Health and safety regulations impose special requirements like radiators which will not burn the elderly person who inadvertently touches one. This adds to the cost of care provision.

But what most distinguishes the cost of care is staff costs. Of course Mr Brown will have had some domiciliary care input but that is costed per hour and made available to users at a subsidized rate in most areas. The costs of care staff are beyond the control of local management. Pay rates are established through national negotiation although an increasing number of authorities have abandoned national scales for locally determined and negotiated rates to secure greater flexibility. The basic costs are compounded by enhancements payable for shift working, night duty, weekend working and uniform costs so that the true hourly rate to the employer may be substantially higher than the basic pay rate. And instead of paying for exactly what he receives, Mr Brown is paying for 24-hour cover and staffing rotas set to accord with legislation and inspection requirements.

Large buildings cost a lot in maintenance. The heating system has to be reliable in order to deliver year-round warmth. The size of residential homes also means that when improvements are required, the capital cost can be heavy and for the private sector loan repayment costs can be high.

These direct costs will constitute around 70 per cent of the total costs, with food 10 per cent, care staff 40 per cent, and maintenance 15 per cent of the total. In addition, there are then administrative costs associated with the record keeping necessary for good standards of care and in the voluntary sector fund-raising costs.

In the public sector, however, the overheads carried by the home will be a substantial element in the unit cost. These comprise a recharge to the home of the cost of the social services departmental support, not only direct line management but a proportion of senior management time, a proportion of the finance function and of personnel costs. These departmental recharges can be almost as high as the direct costs attributable to the residential home but it does not stop there. The council's central functions – the computer system and its maintenance, the central finance function and council-wide personnel policy costs – have to be recharged. The effect is to load a burden on the unit cost of the residential home which makes it appear uncompetitive.

The transfer of homes to the independent sector, whether to a not-for-profit trust or a private provider, can therefore usually be presented as reducing the unit costs of care because it strips out these overheads. But the Mayoral car keeps running and so does the finance and personnel function. The effect therefore can be to drive up the unit costs of those services which remain in-house, making them appear hopelessly uneconomic. Understanding the make-up of costs is therefore essential because any decisions to cease providing a service or to externalize a service have to be taken with a realistic assessment of true savings and identification of those overheads which will remain for the council as a whole. Equally, any assessment of comparative costs has to ensure that one is indeed comparing like with like.

CASE STUDY 12: UNIT COSTS

If the home in which Mr Brown is resident has thirty residents and the total cost taking into account the various factors set out above is £475,000 per annum, what is the unit cost? If a private home two doors down from Mr Brown's home can offer a residential care place at £285 per week, which constitutes the best value for money?

If you think you know the answer to the second question, it is because you have not understood the question! Value for money is not a simple exercise of comparing costs. The quality of care and its suitability for Mr Brown have to be taken into account and set against the price differential.

MARGINAL COSTS

The other factor which has to be examined in looking at comparative costs is the marginal cost. If Mr Brown's home costs £475,000 a year to run when full, what would be the impact of it operating at 75 per cent occupancy through the year? There would be savings on food and some savings on staff. These, however, would not be pro-rata savings. Vacancies rarely arise neatly allowing one to shut down a wing of the home. The likelihood is that all the residential units will be below full capacity and unlike hospital wards one cannot put a resident on a trolley and wheel them to another area with vacancies. Assuming that the savings amount to £45,000, the maintenance costs and the overhead costs remain unchanged, leaving the total cost to be distributed over fewer places, the effect would be to increase the unit cost from £304 per week to £367.

The private sector can use marginal costs as a way of responding to the market more readily than public sector providers. If there is 75 per cent occupancy at the £285 per week rate, the home may be barely profitable. But increases in occupancy have a dramatic effect on profitability. Selling places at a lower rate, say, £270, to take occupancy to 95 per cent, would be worthwhile as the fixed costs and overheads would not increase with the increase in resident numbers. The marginal cost is the true additional cost incurred in food, heating, lighting and power and staffing for each additional resident. In practice, of course, it is by no means this simple. Local authority purchasers drive hard bargains. They know when homes have vacancies. They know the local market in terms of supply and demand. They know what prices have been charged to other purchasers. There is, however, some scope for negotiation to agree a mutually beneficial deal.

For the independent sector price and cost are different. Unit costs are set annually in the public sector and constitute the standard charge payable by any individual meeting the full cost of care. In the independent sector, providers can choose to set a price below their full cost but above their marginal cost in order to get a contribution to their fixed costs as in the example set out. The only equivalent available to the public sector is to sell vacant places at a level above their marginal costs to other local authorities. The more entrepreneurial authorities secure significant income in this way. It does, however, run counter to the defensive culture of local government because it runs the risk that places will not be available to meet an unexpected surge in local demand for places.

ACTIVITY 6.1: COST AND QUALITY

As the lead purchaser of residential care for the elderly you know that there is a shortfall of around twenty places between supply and your projected need for places. You have been planning to buy places as you need them knowing that there is sufficient market capacity. You think you can get the places you need at an average cost of £300 per week although local proprietors claim that the impact of the minimum wage, working hours directive and the Inspection Unit staffing requirements are pushing their costs up.

You receive two approaches from the independent sector. A major national provider has taken over a modern forty-place private home and is offering a three-year contract for twenty places at a fee of £285 per week but you have to guarantee 90 per cent occupancy throughout the period.

A local home owner has invested heavily in refurbishment. A completely redecorated and improved wing is to open next month offering physical standards in excess of those you could normally purchase. The usual rates are £350 but the proprietor says that you could purchase all the places in the wing at a discounted figure of £300. He does not want a guarantee because he knows he will be able to sell the places elsewhere because of the home's reputation but requires all the places to be taken up within six months so he is not carrying vacancies.

Here you have a trade-off between cost, quality and flexibility. How would you approach the analysis?

What these exercises demonstrate is that understanding of how costs are made up does not detract from the need for judgement. Choice in social care is not an arithmetical exercise. Various factors have to be weighed before judgements can be made.

In the section above, the issue of marginal costs and the trading opportunities offered was discussed. The field of costing is littered with terms which may at first seem incomprehensible. The glossary of the financial terms at the end of the chapter is intended to help you through the terminological minefield.

THE THREE Es

The nature of competing claims in this field can be seen by reference to the three Es – economy, efficiency and effectiveness. These were used by the Audit Commission when it was established in 1982 to pursue Value for Money in public spending on local authority services. The remit was subsequently widened to include other areas of public expenditure including health. The three Es were usually presented as if they were a single virtuous concept but the words capture different dimensions of spending and can sometimes lead to different results.

Economy is the delivery of a service or product at the lowest possible cost. Every household and every business is engaged in a constant search for economies – ways of achieving the same outcome at lower cost. The advent of the Internet has revolutionized internal communications within large-scale organizations and created a world of two-finger typists to replace the typing pool. Economies have thus been achieved in running costs by large-scale capital investment in computer equipment. In social care some of the methods used to pursue economies have been rather more basic – sending mail second class post unless essential, cutting out peak-time phone calls – and some have involved the reassignment of functions to lower-paid staff.

The contracting process is designed to secure value for money. Too often the process of preparing detailed service specifications and the time and expense involved in the tendering process are only felt to be justified if savings result. These can be cash savings or the achievement of a better outcome in service terms at the same cost. But economy can be a false prophet if it is pursued in isolation from considerations of efficiency and effectiveness.

Efficiency is securing the maximum possible level of outputs for a given level of inputs. In industrial terms, a plant with 100 employees and equipment worth £250,000 produces 50,000 units. A new manager introduces new processes and achieves 60,000 units. That is a gain in productivity through improved efficiency. If the new manager had instead cut staff by 20 and maintained an output of 50,000 units he would have achieved economies by cutting the wage bill by a fifth and also increased efficiency through increased productivity per staff member. But if production fell by 25 per cent because the whole workforce became demoralized thinking they were next in line for redundancy, he would have achieved economy in terms of the wage bill but at the cost of both reduced efficiency and reduced productivity.

In the context of social care the measures of productivity and efficiency are not always so easy to identify. Domiciliary care offers one example, however. In order to achieve savings, the mileage allowance paid to home care workers in a semi-rural area is withdrawn – an economy. Relying on public transport means, however, that each worker is able to see only three clients a day instead of the average of four previously seen – a loss of efficiency. Every economy proposed has therefore to be weighed against any resultant loss of efficiency as a consequence.

Effectiveness is the measure of whether objectives have been achieved. The Gulf War was effective if the objective was to free Kuwait from Iraqi rule. If the objective was the overthrow of Saddam it was woefully ineffective. Measuring effectiveness in social care is notoriously difficult. Despite the array of indicators and targets which have accompanied the Performance Assessment Framework and Quality Protects, many are proxies for effectiveness rather than true measures. Preparing care plans within a given timescale and giving a copy to the client are examples of good practice rather than checks on effectiveness. Sometimes cost-effectiveness and effectiveness are regarded as synonymous. They are not. If improvement in educational standards to a given level is the objective and can be achieved through an extra 100 hours tuition, deploying 200 hours would not be cost-effective.

Cost-effectiveness is the deployment of the minimum input needed to achieve a given objective. In commissioning services it is cost-effectiveness which one seeks. It combines effectiveness and efficiency. It may produce economies but that is not the priority. Services have to demonstrate that they are cost-effective. That is not a simple matter of comparing costs but also comparing outcomes.

CASE STUDY 13: COST-EFFECTIVE CARE

The care of people with mental health problems provides an example. There are two mental health hostels in the area. One is provided by the NHS. It is staffed by psychiatric nurses supported by care staff. The other hostel is provided by the local authority and is staffed by a similar number of staff but without professional qualifications except for the manager. When established, the target population for the two hostels was different with the NHS hostel catering for more complex needs. The scarcity of hostel places has led to a blurring of criteria and both are used now for similar needs.

Both offer individual care plans but the unit cost of the NHS hostel is 30 per cent higher than the local authority because of the staff mix. Which is the more cost-effective and how would one judge?

Faced with this question one has to find tools for measuring effectiveness and then place a value on the differential change achieved. In commissioning one has to decide if better outcomes are worth the additional cost. For example, if the NHS hostel produced 15 per cent more people moving into independent tenancies and avoiding relapse – is that worth a 30 per cent cost premium? If the increase in independent tenancies was only 5 per cent, would that lead to a different view? Faced with the task of reconciling outcomes against costs, analysts have struggled to develop tools which help to address these thorny value issues.

COST-BENEFIT ANALYSIS

The application of cost-benefit analysis is a variant on cost-effectiveness. This method of economic analysis values both costs and benefits in monetary terms. This raises difficult issues in social care. 'How do you decide how much an increase in the length of a person's life is worth? How do you put a monetary value on freedom from abuse or avoidance of homelessness?' (Byford 2000).

True cost-benefit analysis will examine both direct and indirect costs. Thus in the mental health hostel example the costs would include the loss of productivity and earning power as a result of individuals' mental health problems and the social security costs involved as well as care costs. Similarly complex issues arise in the calculation of benefits which go beyond a narrow issue of the health gain for the individual to look at benefits in terms of tax, employment, impact on family and carers and overall quality of life.

The application of economic techniques to social care is worthy of a book all to itself. It can be fiendishly complex. The purpose of this section is to illustrate that there is no pure scientific technique to assist the commissioner. Judgements, and often value judgements, are integral to the process. What is essential in looking at competitive submissions is to ensure that like is being compared with like, that all elements of the costs of service have been taken into account and that the measurement of outcomes is truly comparable.

Equity

Before leaving this section, Knapp (1995) has argued that a fourth E – equity – should be added to the other three as the proper concern of public policy and any audit of expenditure. Equity was one of the dimensions of quality in Maxwell's typology (1984) discussed in Chapter 7. It is a crucial element in the allocation of scarce resources. This concept of fairness means that people with equal needs should be treated equally. That means that purchasers have to satisfy themselves that the model of service offered by contractors will be fair between different groups of people. One obvious example is the existence of anti-discriminatory clauses in the contract and the establishment of monitoring mechanisms to ensure that these conditions are met. These apply usually to gender disability and ethnicity. But considerations of equity may need to be more wide-ranging.

A provider might offer a better service or a lower-cost service in a middle-class suburb than in a run-down inner city area with problems of vandalism. Arguments about difficulty in recruitment, the high cost of insurance, damage to vehicles, etc. could easily be cited. The onus then shifts to the purchaser to decide whether this constitutes an acceptable variation. Proceeding from a basis of equity – the distribution of equal services to those with equal needs – there can be only one answer. But somewhere in the contract there will need to be recognition that the contractor bears extra costs in delivering the same service to an area with high levels of crime and limited facilities – either by a premium payment or by accepting a price loading across the whole contract.

Looking at tenders

The sections above have illustrated that the task of commissioning and purchasing social care is not as straightforward as finding the cheapest supplier and ordering the service. Even the cost basis on which judgements are made is open to question and the quality of delivery is a vital consideration.

When one has prepared a detailed specification and sought tenders, there is a further difficult task in analysing the returned tenders. However precisely those responsible for the documentation seek to be clear about the way in which they want submissions to be drafted, or figures set out, one of the immutable laws of contracting is that it never quite works as planned. Sometimes figures are not shown where they should be but appear in an appendix; sometimes they are prepared on a different basis to that specified; sometimes they do not add up correctly; sometimes they are omitted pending clarification of an issue raised in the submission.

In responding to tenders there are therefore a number of important safeguards which organizations need to put in place to protect themselves against subsequent action. These include the following:

- A team of people, not one person, to look at the tender returns. This protects the individual against any allegations of partiality. It also means that a collective judgement is brought to bear on quality considerations.
- The tender document should be explicit about how the forms should be completed, the date and time of return, and to whom they should be returned.
- Tender documentation should make it clear that non-compliance with these conditions may lead to disqualification of a tender.
- The tender team should contain both contractual and service expertise.
- Criteria should be set in advance against which tenders will be evaluated.
- Criteria should be both financial and non-financial. In order to promote the trade-off between price and quality and to prevent the dominance of price criteria, it may be helpful to weight the criteria.
- The track record of the provider and their record of delivery should always be a criterion.

COSTINGS IN TENDERS: CAUTIONARY TALES

Everybody who has been involved in selecting contractors will have a disaster story. But disasters can be powerful learning tools. Local authority A was exploring the remodelling of one of its old people's homes. It invited expressions of interest from design consultancies, and followed this up with presentations from three firms. One was half the price of the other two, and proposed a design which would enable the rebuilding to take place without decanting the existing residents. Given the shortage of residential care places in the area, this was an important consideration. This proposal was from an individual consultant. The other two were from established firms and their higher costs seemed to reflect the organizational overheads which were carried in their costs. The decision was made to award the contract to the individual.

His first thoughts were imaginative, sensitive to the needs of residents, and well presented. Enthusiasm ran high in the home as he began a series of consultation meetings with residents. Then one day in the post the Director of Social Services received an anonymous letter about the consultant. The letter contained a press cutting about his conviction for fraud three years earlier and alleged that he had misrepresented past performance on projects, and in reality had left a trail of dissatisfied clients in his wake.

An investigation was launched which broadly confirmed the anonymous allegations and the consultant was sacked. He then sued the council for payment for the work undertaken, and the local authority ended by paying a six figure sum and effectively having to start all over again.

The lessons are clear. First, there was no check made on references. The consultant's word about his previous work was accepted. While references may be of limited utility if one is dealing with a large firm with an established reputation for quality, they are essential when dealing with individuals. Second, the decision to appoint was taken by an individual rather than by a group with agreed predetermined selection criteria. Third, the low cost of the tender and its ability to meet departmental requirements blinded the selector to the potential pitfalls with the contractor.

Another example comes from domiciliary care. Chapter 3 looked at the proposed separation of personal care from the cleaning and shopping tasks in a local authority from a user perspective. While the personal care was delivered in-house, the domestic support services element was tendered. Savings of up to £250,000 were anticipated from this process which would free trained and experienced staff to concentrate on the more highly skilled tasks.

The tender process was complicated as bidders were asked to tender by geographical area so the contracts would be three separate contracts although tenderers could apply for all three. The rationale for this was, first, the domiciliary care market in the area was underdeveloped and some smaller contractors might be able to take on one small contract but not all three and, second, three contracts would offer opportunities for comparison between contractors on both cost and quality.

The tenders came in higher than had been anticipated. Each contract was let to a different provider to promote competition and it was hoped to drive up standards overall. The lowest tenderer of the three was given the largest contract. In the middle of the contract process this tenderer was bought out by a large nationally known organization which seemed to promise greater security and controls.

Anxieties begun during the set-up period before the contract began. Management time was taken up by the merger and systems were not in place. The adequacy of the computer system for rostering and billing purposes was in doubt. And so it proved for when the contractor started, a litany of complaints swamped the Civic Centre. Homes went unvisited, staff changed from day to day, bills were inaccurate, and records were incomplete. Councillors swiftly became involved and after several efforts at remedial action and the serving of a warning notice the contract was terminated after four weeks. The in-house service then had to rescue the area before decisions could be made on reallocation.

Adding up the redundancy costs to the in-house staff displaced by the contract, the costs in the tender process, the opportunity cost of the staff time taken up in the remedial and termination stages, and the cost of reallocating the contract, the episode cost the council money without achieving the improved service it had sought.

What lessons can be learnt from this? First, tenders should be let on the basis of cost and quality but deliverability is a factor which needs to be taken into account. Deliverability means the capacity of the contractor to do the work. A number of factors come into play – the size of the organization, its financial backing, its experience of projects of this size and its experience of information technology. In this instance the failure of the IT system was the critical factor undermining all the efforts of the contractor.

Second, it is crucial to take the right decisions before going out to tender on the size and packaging of the contract. Some market testing to ensure that the tender will attract sufficient interest to give a real choice of providers may also be worthwhile.

Third, a risk assessment should be undertaken before contracts are let to consider everything which might go wrong and sketch out a rudimentary fall-back position. This does not need to be a full contingency plan of the Millennium bug variety, but it needs to address how business can be carried on if systems break down for any reason.

Fourth, in looking at the costs and benefits of any initiative it is important to factor in all the costs. The original review which suggested savings of £250,000 ignored the redundancy costs of in-house staff and was fundamentally flawed as these alone absorbed nearly half the projected savings.

Making changes is a complex and demanding process. Hard thinking before the tender process can save a great deal of subsequent effort.

ACTIVITY 6.2: LOOKING AT TENDERS

This exercise is about tenders, and how to examine them. After reading the three tenders, prepare a list of questions you would want to put to the tenderer, areas where you would seek savings on the tender and identify the risks associated with each submission.

The service for which tenders have been sought is the management and operation of three learning disability hostels in a county. The three hostels are within a 15-mile radius. One is a large old Victorian house which has been converted into a ten-place hostel. There are six men and four women in the hostel with an age range from 24 to 51. The staff consist of a manager, a deputy and a team of six care staff plus a cook and two domestic assistants who also help with meals. The total running costs of the hostel are £325,000 p.a.

The second is a purpose-built unit integrated with a housing development with six residents. It has a small staff team of four who share the cooking and cleaning with residents. The annual running costs are £172,000.

The third is the largest unit with eighteen places but the building is divided into three six-bedded units which come together for communal activities but take meals separately except on special occasions. The three units cater for medium dependency, high dependency and high dependency with behavioural problems respectively. The total staff team is a manager, a deputy and three unit heads with four care staff in the medium dependency unit, six in the high dependency unit and eight in the complex needs unit. In addition there are four catering and domestic staff and an administrative assistant. The staff bill is £494,000 and the annual running costs are £698,500.

The County Council believes that social care should be about enabling rather than direct provision and is divesting itself of directly managed services as swiftly as it can.

The service specification stressed the vulnerability of residents, the need for a range of activities and close links with carers. It also said that the council was looking for savings on the overall cost of £1.195m.

Three tenders have been received. Tender A is from a voluntary organization with expertise in learning disability care. It runs several hostels in neighbouring local authorities. It has an annual turnover of £7 million. The tender has been prepared by the organization's Business Development Manager.

The tender is for a combined running cost for the service of £1.081 million. Savings of £45,000 are proposed in management costs by having one overall service manager for the three hostels with two managers being displaced. Savings of £55,000 are proposed on other staff costs by aligning the conditions of service of the existing staff with those of the voluntary organization. Savings of £75,000 are proposed on supplies and services including food costs by bringing the cost base in line with that of the voluntary organization. Savings of £150,000 are proposed on central overhead costs. An overhead charge of 10 per cent is proposed as a contribution to the central services of the organization. Extra expenditure of £100,000 is planned on day care programmes and activities. While there are other minor variations in the tender, these are the main changes proposed. The contract costs will increase year by year by the retail price index for non-staff costs and by the local government pay increase for staff costs.

Tender B comes from a consortium of parents and staff. One of the parents involved is a merchant banker with experience of management buy-outs. They offer continuity in terms of staffing and organization. The tender cost is £999,000. The group proposes major savings of £175,000 on central overheads and 'stripping out the bureaucracy of the council'. It takes a different approach to Tender A by proposing to delegate procurement of supplies and services to staff in the three homes and believes that savings of £20,000 can be made in this way by giving staff greater freedom. No changes in staff or activities are proposed but close links will be established with local schools and colleges, and with employers so that this is seen as a community venture. A guarantee has been offered that costs will increase only by the retail price index increase for the four years of the contract.

Tender C comes from a private sector company with a good reputation for high quality and innovative models of care. It takes a more radical approach based on links which it has established with a local housing association. Its tender submission is £950,000.

It proposes to make significant savings over the four years of the contract by the closure of the Victorian house within the first year of the contract. It believes that seven of the residents currently in the two larger hostels could be maintained and supported in a group home setting. They would receive housing benefit and the care provider would then top up the care element by employing off-site staff to support the residents. The total cost of this for the seven residents is estimated at £95,000 but savings of £325,000 would accrue from closure of the Victorian house.

While three places overall would be lost in this pattern of care, the tender believes that this can be covered by normal levels of turnover among the existing residents. It points to a fall in the level of demand for hostel care as more options open up for those with learning disabilities.

Tender C, like the others, anticipates savings on central overheads and puts these as £110,000. It also anticipates further savings on the staff bill at the two remaining hostels by moving away from national terms and conditions, and in particular shift payments for anti-social hours of £75,000.

The expenditure proposed on provisions is higher by £35,000 than existing costs but the tenderer includes reference to the quality of the meals and a well-known TV chef as consultant. A charge of 13 per cent equivalent to £130,000 is proposed to cover all administrative, management, personnel and finance services from the national HQ.

Work out where the weaknesses are in each proposal. Then write out your questions for each tenderer and compare your questions with those in Chapter 9.

A further word of caution: public sector procurement is governed by strict regulations designed to eliminate any temptation or undue influence on those making decisions. Procedures therefore have to be fair to all parties. The room for post-tender negotiation is less than individuals would have if negotiating about the costs of a house extension. Asking all providers to review their catering costs would be acceptable. Asking one provider only to do so would not. The National Lottery is a good example of an aggrieved bidder seeking judicial review on the grounds that the Lottery Commission were not operating on a level playing field.

GLOSSARY OF FINANCIAL TERMS

Capital   expenditure on items which enhance or maintain the value of the asset. This expenditure is usually non-recurring on large items which do not need to be funded each year.

Capital employed   the total value of the capital involved in the fixed assets of the concern – property, equipment, vehicles.

Capital return   the surplus or profit generated by the business in relation to the capital employed. Increasingly used in public sector finance to assume a rate of return on capital as a measure of efficiency.

Costs   see **direct costs; fixed costs; marginal costs; opportunity costs; recurring costs; unit costs; variable costs.**

Cost-benefit   the analysis of all the costs and benefits of a course of action usually ascribing a monetary value to each. The analysis will include direct, indirect and hidden costs, particularly opportunity costs of any decision.

Cost-effectiveness   the deployment of the minimum input to secure a given objective. Using three people to staff a rota where four were used previously is cost-effective IF the objective of safe care is still achievable with that staffing input.

Direct costs   the costs directly incurred in the provision of a service. This would include staff costs, catering costs and heating costs.

Economy   the delivery of service at the lowest cost.

Effectiveness   the achievement of the desired objective for the service

Efficiency   the maximum level of outputs attainable for a given level of input.

Fixed costs   the costs incurred in providing a service regardless of the level of usage. An empty old people's home is not a nil cost enterprise. Fixed costs are incurred in maintenance, insurance, minimal heating, etc.

Marginal costs   strictly speaking, the costs of providing one additional unit of a service. The costs are therefore those directly attributable to the extra provision. Fixed costs are unaltered if a home has thirty-six or thirty-seven residents; the staff bill may remain the same, but there will be an increase in catering and laundry costs. It is this latter element which constitutes the marginal cost of the service.

Opportunity costs   this is a different concept to the other costs in this section. It captures the cost of lost opportunities. If one decides to open a home for sixteen people instead of twenty-four, there is an opportunity cost in terms of the eight people who may have to stay in hospital or unsatisfactory conditions at home, and in the extra stress borne by their carers. Opportunity costs are important in cost-benefit analysis.

Pricing   the charge levied by the provider for a service. This will need to take into account marginal and fixed costs, the capacity of the provider organization, the nature of the market and possible competition, and the sensitivity of potential demand to price changes.

Recurring costs   these are the costs which recur annually – staff, catering, insurance, etc. – as compared with those initial costs in setting up a service such as building works and recruitment, or one-off items of large capital expenditure such as central heating replacement costs.

Unit costs   the true cost of providing a unit of service for an individual user which will include both fixed and variable costs.

Variable costs   the costs which can vary in line with increases in the level of activity including staff costs, catering costs, etc. as opposed to fixed costs.

KEY POINTS

☐   Unit costs need to be distinguished from marginal costs.

☐   Public sector overhead costs cannot be directly compared with private sector costs – the democratic process has its cost.

☐   Careful thought is needed about the form and packaging of tenders.

☐   Value for money comes from services which deliver objectives effectively and efficiently.

KEY READING

The literature on costing, or that accessible to the non-accountant, is thin. The best introduction comes in three monographs by Bean and Hussey, *Managing the Devolved Budget* (1996), *Costing and Pricing Public Sector Services* (1996) and *Finance for Non-Financial Public Sector Managers* (1997). These provide an excellent summary of key issues in public sector management. A more traditional presentation comes in *Cost Management in the Public Sector* (1994) by Lapsley, Llewellyn and Mitchell.

CHAPTER 7

PURCHASING QUALITY CARE

<h2>OBJECTIVES</h2>

By the end of this chapter you should be able to:

▪ Understand the various dimensions of quality in social care.

▪ Build quality standards into your purchasing policy.

▪ Assess the value of various accreditation models as guarantors of quality.

▪ Know how to monitor and measure quality in the performance of the contract or agreement.

THE DIMENSIONS OF QUALITY CARE

'Damn fine coffee' was the repeated phrase of the enigmatic Cooper in David Lynch's TV series *Twin Peaks*. But what makes for damn fine coffee? Is it the quality of the beans, of the process, of the blender, or the water? Is one person's damn fine coffee undrinkable by some other people in the street? Pirsig summed up the dilemma:

> Quality . . . you know what it is, yet you don't know what it is. But that's self-contradictory. But some things are better than others, that is they have more quality. But when you try to say what the quality is, apart from the things that have it, it all goes poof!
>
> (1974: 184)

Social services managers will often say that they can judge the quality of a residential home the moment they step across the threshold by the layout atmosphere and appearance of the reception area. While hunch and instinct can be useful tools in monitoring visits, they have no place in purchasing. The task of the purchaser is to build these often intangible qualities into the specification. This is even more important in domiciliary care. At least the user, their carer and the care manager have a chance to visit a residential home and form a view before the placement is finalized. In home care the care is unseen and the quality of delivery more difficult to measure.

How, then, can one measure the quality of care? Maxwell identified six dimensions of quality. While he was writing in the context of health care systems (Maxwell 1984), they are equally applicable to social care. The six were as shown below:

1   *Accessibility* to the service user: this is not only physical accessibility in terms of geography, or access to people with disabilities. It also covers the level of public information about the service and how it is made available to users.
2   *Relevance* to the needs of the community: a quality service will meet the priorities of the community. A service in a multi-ethnic community should look and feel very different to that in a middle-class suburb. The staff employed should reflect that broad ethnic mix with suitable language skills to promote access and involvement.
3   *Effectiveness*: a quality service should be able to demonstrate its effectiveness in achieving its objectives. Effectiveness is dealt with in detail in Chapter 6. Here the important aspect is that quality cannot exist in a vacuum. It has to be linked to the ability of a service to deliver what it sets out to achieve.
4   *Equity*: fairness is at the heart of a quality service both in how it is delivered on clear and publicly known criteria and how it is assessed. Treating people with equal needs equally is essential although the individualized nature of assessment in social care sometimes makes this difficult to achieve.
5   *Acceptability*: a quality service is responsive to the user. Frozen meals reheated in a microwave may make good economic sense but for users over 75 who have never possessed a microwave they may be wholly unacceptable. Ways in which services can change to increase responsiveness to users are dealt with in Chapter 5.
6   *Efficiency and economy*: these criteria added to effectiveness constituted the three Es advocated by the Audit Commission in assessing the value for money element of service provision. They were considered in detail in Chapter 6. They are sometimes presented as if they were the only dimensions that mattered and it is important to take the rounded set of dimensions presented by Maxwell into account.

BUILDING QUALITY INTO THE CONTRACT

The starting point has to be the terms of the contract negotiated with the supplier. The standard conditions governing the contract have been dealt with in Chapter 5. The focus of this section is exclusively on quality. A horses for courses approach is required. Quality services in day care, residential care and domiciliary care may have very different characteristics. One thing in common, however, will be a clear focus on meeting the need of the service user. How can that concern be built into the provision of service by a third party?

The approach taken by the purchaser will vary according to the nature of the contract. In some instances a local authority will have a block contract for the provision of a given number of places in a residential or nursing home. There the quality standards will be incorporated in the contract between the authority as purchaser and the home as the provider. Individual placements in residential or nursing homes outside the block contract will often be based on similar provisions to those in the block contract. This may be through use of the preferred provider list or agency policy insisting on standard contractual clauses.

In domiciliary and day care, similar patterns may apply. The authority will usually purchase on a volume basis up to so many hundred hours service from a supplier and will then call that agreement into play as the basis for providing ten hours a week to Miss Smith. Again, the contract will contain the quality standards and monitoring mechanisms sought by the authority.

There are three ways in which contracts can be used to enforce and monitor quality. They can do so by *process* requirements covering vetting procedures, staffing policies, and training policy; by *input* requirements covering staffing levels and rotas; and by *outcome* measures such as user satisfaction, either measured positively through surveys or negatively by complaints monitoring.

Process requirements

Vetting

The time-honoured practice of references is one obvious way of checking the suitability of staff. It is a practice more honoured in the breach than the observance with appointments often made and offered subject to references which are then pursued over the phone in a perfunctory manner. The reason is that few will offer as referees those who know something to their discredit so bland statements about the worth of the applicant have become standard. The attention given to references in local government has begun to shift as a result of more stringent procedures introduced initially in the context of child care following the Warner Report (1992) on selection of residential child care staff. Local authorities are enjoined to take up references prior to offering appointment and to follow up any discrepancies in the application, particularly gaps in the period of employment.

In addition to taking up references, a police check needs to be run to ensure the protection of vulnerable clients. This is established practice in relation to child care following the Warner recommendations but has not been fully implemented in adult services. It can be very time-consuming, delaying urgently needed staff appointments. The protection of vulnerable adults at risk is as important as child protection. Many adults, from the housebound elderly person living alone through to people with disabilities, are prone to abuse whether physical or financial. Establishing the previous employment history of potential staff does not offer complete protection but is a necessary starting point.

It will also be important to check any registers, for example, the Department of Health 'Consultancy index' and the Department for Education and Employment 'List 99', which record the names of teachers and child care staff with convictions or disciplinary action in circumstances which render them unsuitable for employment.

The onus for this is carried by the service provider. What the purchaser needs is reassurance that the systems are in place whereby these checks are carried out properly. This task will be considerably eased by the establishment of the new Criminal Records Bureau. This will eventually incorporate the DfEE and Department of Health lists and provide a one-stop shop for checks.

Training

The great majority of social care staff working in a provider service such as residential day or domiciliary care are unlikely to have any formal qualifications. The purchaser cannot therefore rely on the provider's recruitment of already trained staff as at least some guarantee of quality. Instead the purchaser will look for evidence that training is seen as important by the provider and will seek evidence of the following:

- a training policy
- a training programme for staff, and possibly
- a commitment to get a proportion of staff to National Vocational Qualification (NVQ) Level Two by a fixed date during the contract period

Without entering the minefield of the various qualifications in home care and residential care, a scene which is ever changing, there is a national level of consistency in NVQ standards which is a helpful basis for workforce planning.

In the training policy one would look to see evidence of the resources committed by the organization to training and a commitment to give staff the opportunity to undertake training programmes in the organization's time. In the training programme one would look for a basic induction programme for all staff covering the core skills of lifting and handling, hygiene and the nature of relationship with the service user. It is this last element which is critical in social care but is often overlooked in basic training programmes.

What distinguishes social care from other activities is the level of vulnerability of the person cared for. That imposes special responsibilities on providers to ensure not only the protection of the client but also the appropriateness of the relationship. Putting the service user first means understanding the needs of the user, the part which the service being delivered plays in the overall care plan, listening to the user and being flexible in how the service is delivered. Training can help staff understand where the boundaries lie between employment and friendship. There can be no hard and fast guidance on this area because one wants staff to have qualities of warmth and empathy, not to be distant and impersonal. But staff have to understand that their ability to do the task for which they are employed requires the retention of objectivity about the needs of the client.

The commitment of the provider to training can be measured by the level of budget made available for training and by the time spent on training. In social care one would expect to see at least 2 per cent of the organizational budget and staff time devoted to training and staff development activities. As suggested above, this can be assessed by applying either input measures – budget and time – or outcome measures – the proportion of staff qualified to a given standard.

Input requirements

Staffing

In framing the specification for quality care, staffing levels are a critical area of examination. They are similar to training in one respect. They too are proxy measures for quality. Whereas high staffing levels do not guarantee quality, low staffing levels do put quality care at risk.

Here the purchaser has to draw on experience of comparable services. One of the most powerful arguments for the retention of in-house provision by local authorities has been the importance of retaining the organizational knowledge about staffing levels, rotas, and weekend and unsocial hours cover. Without that direct knowledge local authority purchasers are less able to scrutinize and understand those areas of the provider's approach where the proposed approach to staffing cover may be flawed.

In residential care providers may be able to offer savings compared with local authority-managed services by reducing the level of overheads or by reducing layers of supervision and management. That can offer cost savings for purchasers. What cannot be compromised is the level of staff available for direct care throughout the waking day. The purchaser will therefore look critically at rotas to ensure that there is adequate cover not just in terms of health and safety and registration requirements, but also in terms of the level of activities and interaction with residents which staff can undertake. Has the provider made adequate allowance for sickness cover? What guarantees can the provider offer on continuity of care to support group living arrangements?

In domiciliary care the issue of continuity becomes even more important. The vulnerability of people in their own homes where the contact between worker is invisible to both the purchaser and the provider agency means that care has to be taken to provide reassurance to the service user. That reassurance comes best from continuity and reliability.

Budget

Another important input measure is the scale of investment in particular aspects of service. This could be the size of the training budget or catering budget. It could be the volume of staff time devoted to an activity. Again, purchasers benefit from being able to apply direct experience from in-house services or to use data from benchmarking studies which provide detailed comparative information against which the provider's costs can be tested.

The processes set out above are important in setting minimum standards to which all providers should be expected to sign up. They are usually proxies as they do not purport to measure quality but they are necessary precursors to a quality service.

Outcomes

Outcomes are increasingly the area of examination in social care. Two strands of public policy have come together to produce this emphasis – the focus on users and users' views and the focus on the effectiveness of social care intervention.

In evaluating quality one obvious answer is to ask the service user. Here the consumerist stance first advocated by Griffiths in 1988 can come into play. User surveys are the key to measuring performance. They are used as part of the Joint Review process to assess overall satisfaction of users with levels of service. They can be used as a tool in developing Best Value reviews but their use outside these set-piece events has been surprisingly limited in social services. Yet a simple survey of user views repeated at six-monthly or annual intervals yields important data about how users experience the service, and potential areas for improvement. The old culture of local government has some way to shift before social services departments can have a survey or marketing section without politicians criticizing managers for taking resources from service delivery. Without this, however, it is impossible to measure whether the return on investment is worthwhile.

Where surveys have been carried out, it is noteworthy that the halo effect surrounds the provision of personal care. Satisfaction levels hardly ever fall below 60 per cent. This may be a more eloquent comment on the low expectations of service users and their gratitude for any help than a comment on the quality of the service given. Nevertheless repetition of such surveys on an annual or biennial basis does make it possible to measure shifts over time. While focus groups have been much derided in the political context, they too can offer helpful clues to both purchasers and providers of areas where improvements can be made.

What is more difficult is the measurement of observed quality. By definition in domiciliary care there is no observer of the transaction between worker and client. In residential care so many different elements come into play in measuring quality – food, accommodation, environment, other users, staff – that it is difficult to disaggregate. One area which has been studied is the level of interaction between staff and residents. How many times in the course of the day does a resident have an exchange of conversation with staff? What opportunities are there for creative and imaginative activities beyond the sterility of television – the opiate of residential homes?

One approach to outcomes is to make specified outcomes the key contractual requirement leaving great flexibility for the provider as to how those outcomes are achieved. Some of the targets set in *Quality Protects* for looked-after children are outcome-based. They include a given level of educational attainment measured in GCSEs obtained. Applying this to adult care one could construct outcomes in terms of proportion of those in a mental health hostel moving on to independent living. In learning disability it could be related to the proportion of those in group homes with regular daytime activity at college or in a day centre. In residential homes for old people it might be the proportion of residents able to maintain three or more Activities of Daily Living nine months after admission.

ACTIVITY 7.1: OUTCOME MEASURES

Devise suitable outcome measures for the following:

- A drug rehabilitation residential centre.
- An intensive hospital discharge domiciliary care scheme.
- An adoption service.

BUILDING COLLABORATION ON QUALITY

The material on quality has been presented hitherto as if quality was the exclusive preoccupation of the purchaser. It is not. Providers have not only to win contracts but also to maintain their reputation by delivering a good service once the contract has been let. They will have their own internal quality assurance measures and evidence of the way in which they operate will be a reassurance to purchasers. In social care collaboration and partnership need to extend to the purchaser–provider relationship. This collaboration needs to extend to the definition of quality care. How can that collaboration be developed?

A variety of techniques have been used to bridge the gap between purchaser and provider. Importing a new concept into the language of social care is always difficult. Inevitably the initial reaction was to look for expertise in contracting processes. In most authorities those skills were found in legal services and in housing with its extensive contractual involvement with both construction and building maintenance. As discussed earlier, the combination of legalism and the confrontational model of building contracts where claim and counter-claim are part of the process was not the best model. Authorities were drawn into conflict rather than collaboration and it has taken a long while before this influence has been rolled back. Yet borrowing from models of collaborative relationships between manufacturer and supplier which have characterized Japanese industry, and have increasingly been used in the UK, different models began to emerge.

Williamson summarized the concept as 'working together to improve quality and where possible to add value or achieve cost reductions. It means helping providers to develop by sharing information about likely future needs, encouraging innovation, and providing feedback' (Williamson 1997: 13).

The pure milk of competition can be a powerful influence driving down costs. It presupposes, however, that there is potential supply in excess of the demand. This is not the case in social care. In many areas of work – domiciliary care, specialist residential care, community support services, and hostel provision – there is a limited capacity on the part of providers and an excess of demand. Given the demand it might seem surprising that the market in care has not expanded more rapidly. The reality is that demand is not infinite when it is mediated through community care funding. The scope for creating surplus capacity has been restrained by the *de facto* control of the size of the care market exercised by social services holding purse-strings dictated by a cash-limited budget.

Commissioners and purchasers have therefore to stimulate the market. Where the objective is to increase the range of providers, or to encourage existing providers to expand their capacity or move into new areas of services, they may choose a different approach. Among the options which could be considered are:

1   A conference for all potential providers which can serve as an information day about what the authority is hoping to achieve as well as helping to clarify the potential models of delivery. A conference on meals on wheels, for example, might develop different options from frozen meals and the supply of a microwave for reheating through to use of surplus capacity in a local school kitchen to prepare meals, and different options for the delivery of meals from the traditional vans through to pizza-style delivery on motorcycles.

2   A request for proposals in which the ideas of potential providers are canvassed in advance of any formal tendering procedures. This is a more formal procedure because it is the precursor to a selection process. It will work only if the authority is very clear about what it wants to achieve and sets certain core standards.

3   Draft service specifications can be used to seek comments from providers before they are formally adopted. This has significant advantages in weeding out some of the redundant conditions that can easily creep into documentation. Specifically it allows providers the chance to query quality standards if they believe these to be unrealistic, unmeasurable or undeliverable. This can save disputes at a later stage.

4   A single provider can be selected and then purchaser and provider work together to develop the details of the service. This involves the provider in shaping the final details of the service to ensure that it meets the needs of the purchaser.

The options set out above are not mutually exclusive. What they illustrate is a variety of techniques which can be used to move to a collaborative model of purchasing.

ACTIVITY 7.2: QUALITY STANDARDS

You have recently been appointed as the lead purchaser for drug and alcohol services in the area. There are a number of drug agencies providing residential rehabilitation programmes, outreach services and follow-up counselling. There is, however, a dearth of services for people with alcohol problems. The NHS has a long waiting list for referral of those with serious drinking problems. There have recently been a number of high profile child protection cases in which alcohol has been a major issue so the Director is keen to develop some better service for those with long-term alcohol dependence.

There is one agency currently working in the area which specializes in drug work but claims it can offer an alcohol service. There is a specialist alcohol service providing drop-in and structured counselling in the neighbouring area.

- How would you go about developing a service?
- What tactics would you adopt to involve providers?
- What quality standards would you be looking for in relation to the service?

Borrowing from the commercial sector again the jargon phrase is relationship management. That covers all the interfaces of the organization with funders, politicians, stakeholders, customers, competitors and suppliers. But a crucial element is the relationship with suppliers where industry is trying new approaches. The Andrew Alliance promoted by BP in the construction of a new oil platform for the North Sea drew together suppliers of components, construction firms, project managers, cost and quality managers, in a regular network to develop a holistic view of the project. Instead of each partner delivering their bit of the task to standards, the Alliance enabled them to share the critical impact on the total project of delays in the supply chain. The end result was a project delivered ahead of time and under the estimated cost – an outcome of sufficient rarity in construction to warrant study! It illustrates the potential benefits of a more constructive approach to the procurement process.

An element in that is trust. Some ways in which one can begin to build trust were set out above. Trust does not come naturally. It has first to be built and that takes time. It has then to be sustained. Local authorities start from the legacy of the period before the community care reforms which was

> characterised by suspicion and mistrust. The belief among local authorities was that home owners in the private sector were often motivated purely by profit maximisation. This motivation was widely thought to be inappropriate in view of the general perception among local authorities – under whatever political control – that 'social care is different.' As such market mechanisms, and especially the pursuit of profit, were widely regarded not only as inappropriate but as unacceptable.
>
> (Hardy and Wistow 2000: 56)

Hardy and Wistow (2000) identify two kinds of mistrust – competence mistrust and goodwill mistrust. The former was mutual. Just as local authorities doubted the managerial ability of some voluntary and private providers, so too did those providers doubt the ability of those in local government to deal with commissioning tasks of which they had little experience. That doubt was compounded by the level of turnover in the staff in commissioning roles, itself militating against the development of trust.

The goodwill element was lacking in many local authority staff who found it difficult to reconcile a profit ethos with caring tasks and were deeply suspicious of cost-cutting to the detriment of users. That was reciprocated by many providers who were convinced that local authorities favoured in-house providers both in the application of registration and inspection procedures, and in relation to potential competition.

The Audit Commission noted 'social services departments typically have adversarial relationships with the independent sector' (1997: 66). Although Hardy and Wistow think that this judgement was too harsh, they note that :

> By 1995/6 local authorities had travelled an enormous distance in terms of understanding, acceptance and competence in managing and developing the emerging quasi-markets. There was . . . a transformation in the degree to which local authority members and officers acknowledged the need to establish collaborative relationships with independent sector providers in the private as well as the voluntary and not-for-profit sectors
>
> (Hardy and Wistow 2000: 59)

NATIONAL STANDARDS

That new model of collaborative relationship has been reflected in the full engagement of the independent sector in the development of national standards. This has to be seen in the context of the broad agenda of the Labour Government to secure greater consistency across the country. This has been expressed largely in the context of health care as the postcode lottery whereby whether a patient receives an expensive drug may depend as much on the policies of the health authority and its financial position as clinical need. Similarly with charges in local authority services, the Audit Commission drew attention to the wide and unacceptable variations in charging policy for domiciliary care (Audit Commission 2000).

One way to address this is the development of national care standards. The government is pursuing a twin-track approach in relation to this objective. It is establishing a new body, the National Care Standards Commission, which will be responsible for securing the consistent application across the country of agreed standards. The Commission will be responsible for the registration and inspection function currently held by local authorities. The second strand is the development for a number of care groups of national standards which will be recommended to service providers and to purchasers.

Registration and inspection have been a long-running source of contention between local authorities and the independent sector. First, local authorities were not initially subject to inspection in respect of their own services. Second, while it was regarded as good practice to submit in-house services to external inspection, they were not subject to the same timescales for improvement as their independent sector counterparts. Third, the standards set were very different between different geographical areas. At one time the Isle of Wight refused to register any homes for the elderly in excess of thirty people while in other parts of the country large developments up to one hundred people were proceeding unchallenged. Finally, the Director of Social Services as the person responsible for the registration unit was viewed as less than even-handed in the application of inspection by virtue of the element of competition between in-house and independent sector services.

To address some of these concerns in 1995 the government asked Chief Executives of local authorities to undertake an annual review of inspection in each authority to satisfy the council and the government that an even-handed approach was being taken to the application of inspection. Lay members were added to the inspection team. Advisory committees incorporating providers were established. While these measures have improved transparency, wide variations have remained between authorities in the approach taken to registration. The new legislation is designed to create a single body responsible for the registration and inspection function applying a consistent national approach and consistent criteria.

It is not yet wholly clear whether the national standards will be minimum, for example, compliance with space standards, provision of assisted baths, staffing levels, etc., or whether an attempt will be made to secure compliance with the good practice standards which constitute the other strand of policy development. Here the scope for conflict with the independent sector is real. To take one example, the standards developed by the Centre for Policy on Ageing for residential homes suggest a minimum of 12 square metres as the space standard for single rooms – a significant increase both on the minimum of 9 square metres now in force and the 10 square metres recommended as good practice. The Chief Executive of the National Care Homes Association protested at the acceptance of this standard which she regarded as sounding the death knell for large numbers of small homes run by nurse-proprietors. The timescale for implementation has now been extended to 2007.

The attempt to produce consistency in the application of good practice through standards is an interesting process. It has been inclusive with many organizations and individuals playing a part in the development of the National Service Framework for mental health, the standards for work with older people and standards for domiciliary care. The three models, however, have worked differently. The mental health framework was the product of a working group informed by a broadly based national reference group. The work on the elderly is the product of a working group jointly chaired by the Chief Inspector of Social Services. The standards on domiciliary care were produced by a working group under the auspices of the Joint Initiative on Community Care, a coalition of organizations involved in the delivery of care.

The JICC model seeks to distil national standards from a database of approved provider schemes and voluntary registration schemes for domiciliary care providers. Provider organizations have therefore had a major input into the development of the standards. The draft standards cover five areas:

- core values such as respect for the dignity and privacy of the user
- business viability
- health and safety
- human resources including staffing levels and training programmes
- operational procedures and practice

To strengthen the utility of the standards for providers, each standard is cross-referenced against the appropriate National Vocational Qualification standard.

The difficulty with these documents is twofold. First, they tend to be couched at a level of generality which reduces their impact. Take this example from the standards for carer support developed by the Kings Fund: 'services should provide information which is comprehensive, accurate and appropriate, accessible and responsive to individual needs' (Banks 1997: 23). Nobody could disagree with this standard. It is, however, aspirational rather than something which one could require as a quality standard in a contract. Providers might respond that they aspire to meet the quality standards laid down by the Kings Fund but as a true measure it leaves something to be desired.

Second, the standards are codes of practice to be followed where possible. They do not have a real and immediate impact on the care received. It is those outcomes which have really to be measured – how the care felt to the recipient. Was it timely, courteous, respectful, useful? There is a danger that process becomes dominant to the exclusion of that focus on outcomes. The purchaser has to ensure that codes and standards are seen for what they are – proxies (sometimes useful proxies) for quality.

The national service frameworks now being developed for aspects of health and social care including mental health and the care of the elderly are rigorous in differentiating those standards which are mandatory and derived from statute or regulations, and those which are recommended good practice. Equal rigour is shown in identifying the type of evidence required to meet the standard. This will be a great assistance to the National Care Standards Commission in its task of securing consistency.

ACTIVITY 7.3: QUALITY MEASURES IN CONTRACTS

Based on what you have read about quality, including the dimensions of quality, the development of national standards and the approved provider lists, how would you approach quality in purchasing a support service for those with mental health problems living in the community? What quality measures would you look for and how would you seek to ensure that they were fulfilled? Specifically, what would you want in the contract, what would you want in overall performance assessment and monitoring, and what would you include in a code of conduct?

ACCREDITATION MECHANISMS

In addition to the development of national standards and new approaches to partnership in contracts, there is a third group of measures which need to be considered by prospective purchasers. This is the rapidly developing field of accreditation.

Accreditation is a process whereby providers submit themselves to independent assessment of their overall performance by an external agency. It thus offers purchasers an external and independent validation of quality and can be a powerful marketing tool for providers. The concept of audit has broadened beyond the accountancy-based scrutiny of the books and accounts of an enterprise to include a broader view of performance including all operational systems. Audit is one way of describing the benefits of accreditation because it identifies where there are shortfalls in the processes used – possibly a lack of written procedures causing some confusion about roles and responsibilities, possibly inadequate attention to risk management.

Accreditation which confers the right to use the appropriate strap line like Investor in People or possessor of ISO 9000 is usually offered by a not-for-profit organization. Any summary of key accreditation bodies is likely to omit some as this is a rapidly developing field but among the major bodies are the following:

- *British Standards Institute*: this is a well-established national organization which has developed British standards for a wide range of industries and commercial undertakings. It is recognized not only in the UK but also in Europe and increasingly its standards are aligned with European standards. Unlike some accreditation schemes, securing ISO 9000/1/2/3 is not a matter of subscribing to motherhood and apple pie aspirational standards. It is a validation of the quality assurance systems within the organization. It requires quality assurance systems not only to cover procedures and processes within the organization but also the type and structure of the organization, the use of resources, customer liaison, and relationships with sub-contractors.

  Although ISO recognition is highly prized, it is something of a misnomer for what are recognized and validated are the quality assurance processes in force, not compliance with standards. The ISO standard takes time to achieve and is renewable annually.

- *Investors in People*: this accreditation scheme is supported by the Department of Trade and Industry and concentrates on the use of human resources. It has four elements: top management commitment to the improvement of standards of training and skill; a plan to review training and development needs regularly; action to develop employees throughout their employment career; and evaluation to improve future effectiveness. It is a paper-driven system of accreditation based on clear written procedures, job descriptions, quality standards and staff development. It has been widely used in the hospitality industry and increasingly in care homes to demonstrate the commitment of the provider to improving the quality of staff. The strength of the IIP award undoubtedly lies in its training commitment. It has been criticized as over-reliant on documentation.

- *Organisational Audit*: the Kings Fund audit has now been retitled the Quality Management Initiative (nothing stays the same for very long in the quality business). This unit has pioneered the concept of accreditation in the health and social care sector. It has built upon extensive work in organizational audit in the hospital context, but has been applied by the unit to community services. A review team from the unit visits the authority under review and also develops substantial documentation of policies and procedures. The time commitment is substantial for the care provider and as yet the Audit has not succeeded in securing universal recognition within health care for its standards and reviews. The extension to community-based services has also been criticized as a transplant of one method to a different setting, which has not been wholly happy.

- *Business Excellence model*: this approach now adopted by the European Foundation for Quality Management is based on an analysis of process. It builds on the deconstructionist enthusiasm of business process re-engineering. It breaks the work of the organization into discrete processes and then seeks to build them together in a more coherent way. It does so by engaging staff within the organization to think about why they do things, how they do things and how they know when they have done things well. The organization's progress to business excellence is judged against nine criteria. These are leadership (the top management commitment as required by Investors in People); policy and strategy based on relevant information; people management with emphasis on communication and staff development; resource management to focus on the efficient use of what is available; processes with an emphasis on continuous improvement to drive change; customer satisfaction with regular monitoring; people satisfaction in terms of staff satisfaction; impact on society; and business results – the degree to which the organization has met its objectives.

  The aim is to secure business processes which will deliver excellence. Its strength lies in its engagement with creativity and the scope to change processes and systems. What it does not wholly avoid is the sense that a pre-ordained model is being sold to the user.

- *Balanced scorecard*: this approach is designed to link strategy, plans and performance measurement. Although not a formal accreditation system, it is sometimes used as an alternative to them. It takes a five-step approach. The first step is the establishment of overall strategic goals and the second is the identification of key actions required to achieve these goals (an alternative description of these first two steps might be strategic and operational objectives). As a third step these initiatives are then reviewed from four different perspectives: the customer, continuous improvement, financial and internal business processes with actions for each perspective. Fourth, performance measures are identified for each action. The distilled performance measures then constitute the scorecard which will contain the actions, the performance measure, the target, and the initiatives underway to achieve the target.

All these approaches and the many others from which one can choose have their strengths and weaknesses. They are almost invariably time-consuming and managers have to decide whether the outputs justify the resource commitment of time and money. To purchasers however they signal, first, that the provider wants to demonstrate a commitment to quality and has backed that with an investment of resources, and, second, they demonstrate that quality assurance processes are in place within the provider organization. This can lead to a relaxation of the quality measures which the purchaser would otherwise have sought to insert in the contract. It is therefore essential that the data generated for accreditation agencies should be made available to the purchaser on request.

KEY POINTS

☐   Contracts can be used to reinforce quality.

☐   Collaborative relationships with providers can help to build partnership work on quality.

☐   National standards and service frameworks are being developed for all care groups.

☐   Accreditation mechanisms can help to reinforce quality in provider services.

☐   The focus needs to remain on outcomes and not process.

KEY READING

There is a rich literature on quality. Publications range from the simple workbook or manual to the thoughtful reflective analysis of the place of quality in social care. At the workbook end of the spectrum are *Quality Assurance in Social Care Agencies* (1992) in which Cassam and Gupta describe the introduction of quality to Norfolk Social Services and *Quality Assurance in Social Care* (1998) in which Ellis and Whittington provide useful exercises for those with the task of focusing on quality. *Performance Review and Quality in Social Care* (1994) is a wider-ranging text edited by Connor and Black. An international perspective and some thoughtful analysis is offered in a publication by Evers *et al.*, *Developing Quality in Personal Social Services* (1997).

CHAPTER 8

NEXT STEPS IN COMMISSIONING

OBJECTIVES

By the end of this chapter you should be able to:

▪ Understand the drive for change in commissioning social care.

▪ Identify the new skills likely to be required.

▪ Appreciate the obstacles in meeting the government's agenda.

▪ Identify the continuity in public policy on user empowerment, contracting and performance management.

ACHIEVEMENTS AND FAILURES

Despite the view that social services departments have failed, which is current within government, they have some remarkable achievements. The delivery of social care in the past decade has followed the prescription set out in the Griffiths Report in 1988. They have developed a mixed economy of care with a growing share of total expenditure going on the independent sector. They have achieved a shift in their role from one of service delivery to one of enabling. They have seen the commissioning and purchasing role strengthened through the delivery of services under contract. They have seen these changes delivered with an effective capping of the social security spend on long-term care which was the primary driver for the changes set out in the Griffiths Report. All this has been achieved without major structural change. That period of relative stability is at an end. The pace of change is quickening. Whether the direction of change will be greatly altered remains an open question.

The National Health Service has been a touchstone issue for the Labour Party since its inception in 1948. The problems of the NHS were a significant factor in the electoral success of 1997. Despite additional investment the failure to secure demonstrable improvement in the quality of health care has been a source of great frustration to successive Secretaries of State for Health. In a vivid phrase the NHS Plan (2000) captured this frustration: 'The NHS is a 1940s' system operating in a 21st century world.'

Why do the problems of the National Health Service matter to the future pattern of social care? There are three reasons:

1   structural change is seen as a legitimate solution to perceived problems
2   local government is mistrusted as a vehicle for delivering efficient services
3   the failures of social care in dealing with delayed discharges are exaggerated and seen as contributing to the problems of the NHS

THE MIRAGE OF STRUCTURAL SOLUTIONS

The NHS has suffered from the misplaced belief that rearranging the deckchairs will stop the *Titanic* from sinking. Throughout the second half of its existence the National Health Service has seen reorganization follow reorganization in quick succession. A cynical view might be that it is easier to reorganize than to resource adequately. While the level of resources is always a political issue, only recently has the government responded with an unparalleled injection of new money far in excess of that required to meet inflationary pressures.

In the febrile period before the publication of the NHS Plan the Prime Minister was quoted as expressing interest in the links between health and social services in Northern Ireland as a model which deserved further investigation for the rest of the United Kingdom. The NHS Confederation was quick to seize an opening and launched a paper proposing a fully integrated health and social care model for consideration by the action teams drawing up the NHS Plan. While the final version of the Plan was silent on integration, there are a number of phrases which suggest this was a matter of regret rather than choice:

> for the first time local health services and local social services will be brought closer together in one organization
>
> (NHS Plan 2000: 15)

> the old divisions between health and social care need to be overcome
>
> (ibid.: 70)

> in future social services will be delivered in new settings, such as GP surgeries, and social care staff will work alongside GPs and other primary and community health teams as part of a single local care network
>
> (ibid.: 71)

> the outdated institutional barriers between health and social services which have got in the way of people getting the care they need when they need it.
>
> (ibid.: 73)

The Plan contains proposals for integrated Mental Health Trusts and Care Trusts but stopped short of recommending wholesale change. Despite a growing recognition that organizational change is wasteful of both time and resources, diverts energy and attention which should be directed to service improvement, and makes organizations inward-looking, subsequent ministerial statements indicate enthusiasm for further changes.

In truth, the evidence from Northern Ireland is at best ambiguous. There are examples of innovation and creative use of the potential for joint working in domiciliary support services and Home from Hospital schemes. But there are also examples of community resources being hijacked to meet deficits in the acute sector, and of institutional solutions being accorded a higher priority than in other parts of the United Kingdom. Despite a significantly higher level of per capita expenditure on health and social care than other parts of the UK, the social care services remain patchy (Bamford 1990: 135–9; McCoy 2000).

Structural change is appealing to politicians seeking to make a difference. It does not, however, offer a quick fix to the problems. Structures work because of the people working within them. Securing their commitment, their morale and their enthusiasm will make even the most cumbersome structure work. Without that support the most efficient structure imaginable will founder.

MISTRUST OF LOCAL GOVERNMENT

Until 1948 local authorities had responsibility for the provision of community health services. Until 1974 the Director of Public Health worked for the local authority. The gap between health and local government is therefore relatively recent.

The NHS Plan contains proposals to strengthen the democratic accountability of health care providers by giving local authorities the power to scrutinize the NHS. 'Chief Executives of NHS organizations will be required to attend the main local authority scrutiny all-party committee at least twice annually if requested' (NHS Plan 2000: 94). The scrutiny committees are also to be given powers currently held by the Community Health Councils to refer major planned changes to NHS services to an Independent Reconfiguration Panel.

This new responsibility challenges the assertion that there is a distrust of local government. Certainly it is a welcome reinforcement of local government in its community leadership role. The continuing mistrust, however, is over the managerial capability within local government to bring about changes.

In contrast to the National Health Service which is directly managed, local government is less open to ministerial priorities. Different political perspectives and different local priorities may divert resources away from ministerial preferences. The degree to which Ministers have sought to control the way in which local education authorities spend the additional resources allocated by government reflects this frustration over the lack of direct control. The poor quality of some local authority leaders and a series of corruption scandals led to the imposed discipline of Best Value but doubts remain about the ability of local government to respond to the timescale and magnitude of change wanted by government.

SOCIAL SERVICES FAILURES

The list of achievements in the first paragraph of this chapter is substantial. Yet a sense of failure surrounds social care, or at least social services departments. Paul Boateng, Minister of State at the Home Office talking about the new Children's Fund, expressed incredulity that social services might have a leading role in the management of the Fund: 'They have let down children year upon year. Now that's beginning to change. But the notion that we can just leave it to the social services is fanciful' (Rickford 2000). The succession of child abuse cases and abuse in residential child care has dangerously eroded not only public confidence but also the confidence of ministers.

As a result, social care is blamed for things beyond its responsibility. The NHS Plan with its description of delayed discharges or bed blocking is a good illustration of the process. Bed-blocking is cited as an example of

> [the] rigid institutional boundaries which can mean the needs of a patient come a poor second to the needs of the individual service. On one day in September last year 5500 patients over 75 and over were ready to be discharged but were still in an acute hospital bed: 23% awaiting assessment; 17% waiting for social services funding to go to a care home; 25% trying to find the right care home; and 6% waiting for the right care home package to be organised. Almost three quarters were not getting the care they needed because of poor coordination between the NHS and other agencies . . . The 1948 fault line between health and social care has inhibited the development of services shaped around the needs of patients.
>
> (NHS Plan 2000: 30)

This passage is worth close textual analysis. First, it appears to repudiate the current organizational pattern for health and social care as a rigid fault line getting in the way of services for patients. Second, it uses a snapshot picture of elderly patients in acute beds to argue that they were not getting the right care because of poor coordination. Third, that poor coordination is ascribed (implicitly) to social services as all the statistics quoted relate to social services responsibilities. Finally, it betrays a total mis-comprehension of what good community care is about, subordinating everything to the priority of getting elderly people out of acute beds.

It constitutes one of the most extraordinary passages to appear in a major government document especially when one looks in detail at the statistics. The 23 per cent awaiting assessment may be a valid criticism although without more detailed analysis it is not possible to know. Had social services been notified? How long had the wait been for assessment? Is the delay while community alternatives are fully explored? The 17 per cent waiting for funding is also not quite what it seems. Social services funding comes from council taxpayers. It is cash limited. Budgets have to be managed and the responsible use of resources for long-term care has been a success story. There cannot be a blank cheque for placements the moment a patient is ready to move on without compromising that budget management.

Most bizarre of all is the suggestion that the 25 per cent waiting for the right care home is a failure of coordination. The statutory direction on choice gives people the right to choose a care home within the financial limits set by the authority. Patients should not be shunted out of acute beds without the opportunity to visit the care home in which they may be placed and possibly to see others before making a decision which may be for the rest of their life. And the 6 per cent waiting for the right care package are worth the wait if the care package prevents them from being readmitted within days because of the poor support available at home.

What is really disturbing about this section is the mind set it illustrates which pays such scant attention to the rights of users, is unaware of their statutory right to choose, and is focused exclusively on the use of acute beds. A health care system should be about health and care, not about acute beds.

THE NHS PLAN

The way in which the government proposes to address the fault line between health and social care is spelt out in the NHS Plan. In addition to the usual array of targets and joint plans, the specific proposals are:

- Partnership agreements are to be made mandatory rather than on the permissive basis on which they had been introduced in April 2000.
- Care Trusts covering health and social care responsibilities are to be introduced on a permissive basis to commission and to be responsible for all local health and social care.
- Mental Health and social care trusts are to be established to secure the integration of local services.

Partnership agreements were introduced by the Health Act 1999. They were designed to promote joint working through pooled budgets, lead commissioning and integrated provision between health and social services. The partnership agreements were voluntary although potentially ambitious in scope: 'the partnership . . . can include all health related local authority functions such as social services, housing and education functions, and community and acute health services' (Department of Health 2000b).

The NHS Plan proposes the replacement of voluntary partnership arrangements by a mandatory requirement for partnership. Although this could be relatively modest, for example an agreement that all substance misuse services would be commissioned by one or other authority, the Plan talks about a radical redesign of the whole care system including the co-location of 'social care staff alongside GP's and other primary and community health teams as part of a single local care network' (NHS Plan 2000: 71).

Co-location is not a new idea. Social work attachments in primary care have existed for over a quarter of a century. They do not require a partnership agreement and they do not guarantee success. Some of the difficulties with co-location were discussed in Chapter 7.

The thrust to partnership working is to be reinforced by two Performance Funds (a NHS fund rising to £500 million a year by 2003/4 and to start in April 2001, and a social services fund of £50 million a year starting in 2002). The existence of separate funds with separate start dates is hardly a striking example of partnership working within the Department of Health!

The focus of these incentives is to be intermediate care in the first instance. This reflects the over-riding priority of the plan which is to ensure that acute beds are used for those in need of urgent treatment. The Plan contains a template of the services required:

- rapid response teams providing emergency care at home and thus preventing unnecessary hospital admissions
- intensive rehabilitation services usually sited in hospitals
- recuperation facilities through short-term care in a nursing home or other accommodation
- local one-stop services in primary care linking social care and health care
- integrated home care teams supporting people when discharged from hospital

This pattern of provision is not new. Many of the measures have been developed to cope with winter pressures in recent years. What is new is the intention that a comprehensive network of services should be rolled out in each area.

It presents formidable challenges to commissioners in terms of the timescale for change, securing premises, establishing protocols for joint working, agreeing leadership roles in multi-professional teams, and developing truly integrated working.

Care Trusts were the surprise element in the Plan. They are defined as a 'new level of primary care trusts' and as 'new single multi-purpose legal bodies to commission and be responsible for all local health and social care' (NHS Plan 2000: 73). Social services powers would be delegated by local authorities to the Care Trust. The basis is intended to be voluntary where there is a joint agreement at local level that this is the best way to deliver better care services. But 'where local health and social care organisations have failed to establish effective joint partnerships – or where inspection or joint reviews have shown that service are failing – the Government will take powers to establish integrated arrangements through the new Care Trust' (ibid.).

This is a curious disjunction. The emphasis on voluntary agreement is right. Delegation by a local authority to a new body will require a high degree of mutual trust and understanding. Yet it is proposed to impose Care Trusts where the organizations are failing to work together – a recipe for compounding the problems rather than solving them.

The Minister of Health John Hutton told *Community Care* that he expected all social care to be delivered by care trusts within five years (*Community Care* 2000c, 9–15 November 2000). This makes the notion of voluntarism highly suspect as local authorities are unlikely *en masse* to wish to divest themselves of their responsibilities.

The Care Trusts could be geographically based on local authority boundaries or they could be care-based on services to the elderly. They present a formidable challenge to commissioners where boundaries of the primary care trusts and local authorities are not coterminous. They will require the construction of new joint planning machinery. At present most joint discussion takes place between the health authority and the local authority. Joint Consultative Committees – the bodies established in 1974 to coordinate work between health and social services – came to an end in 2000 but have often been replaced by Partnership boards to review the totality of the inter-relationship. These boards composed of local authority councillors and health authority members are not likely to be an effective vehicle for managing service delivery.

The intention is that Care Trusts will combine with existing primary care trusts to deliver services. This means a new set of relationships which will be rendered more difficult by the strange management structure which the Department of Health has put in place for primary care trusts. While the non-executive members of trust boards are lay people, there is another body, called the Executive of the trust, which is responsible for day-to-day management. This is chaired by a GP and must have a majority of GPs. The Chair of the Executive receives a higher level of payment than does the Chair of the Primary Care Trust, which is an eloquent comment on the respective power of the two posts.

The historical suspicion between social care and health derives from two primary sources – the fear of medical domination and the limited attention which medicine has paid to the social environment. The tension between the medical and social model is particularly acute for users. Despite the intention of the NHS Plan to put patients and users at the heart of the service, the entrenched position for GPs within primary care trusts will create anxiety about how clearly focused they will be on users. The governance structure for Care Trusts – as distinguished from primary care trusts – is not yet clear but the British Medical Association is the most formidable trade union in the land and will strive to secure a major degree of influence for GPs within the new arrangements.

This potential struggle has implications for commissioners who will have to reconcile the divergent interest of stakeholders and, even more difficult, the different values of the stakeholders. Care Trusts will have many professional interest groups and the task of creating integrated care delivered on a multi-disciplinary basis. Creating an agreed vision will not be easy.

Mental health and social care trusts are the third proposal for organizational change within the NHS Plan. The information provided is remarkably limited. The Plan states baldly that 'to ensure that health and social care provision can be properly integrated locally, statutory powers will be taken to permit the establishment of combined mental health and social care trusts' (ibid.: 122). The implication is that this again will be permissive rather than mandatory although given the enthusiasm for structural change it may well follow partnership agreements in a rapid shift from voluntary to compulsory.

The links with local government in the new mental health Care Trusts will be very much weakened. Mental health trusts tend to cover a number of local authorities and the influence of any single authority will be much less.

The absence of detail means that it is not clear whether this is offered as an example of a care-group based Care Trust or whether these trusts are regarded as different in kind from the slightly more developed proposal for Care Trusts.

ISSUES FOR COMMISSIONERS

These proposals have been covered in some detail because they are the direction of the future. With minor modifications and almost certainly very much more slowly than the NHS Plan envisages, they are likely to create a far more diversified pattern of commissioning social care than has previously been the case. This raises the possibility of a very confused pattern. It will certainly make the performance assessment frame-work for social services redundant as comparability will no longer be possible because of the different patterns of service delivery. The problems for commissioners are, however, more profound. They are how to deal with the end of separation between commissioning and providing responsibilities, and how to establish a shared value base for service delivery.

Commissioning and providing

The separation of these functions has been central to the evolution of both health and social care throughout the period since the 1990 NHS and Community Care Act. The first chapter of this book set out the background to the separation as ministers sought to shift from provider-led services to ones focused on the needs of users and carers.

The separation has created some problems particularly when interpreted as holy writ in structural terms but the mixed economy of care would not have developed as it has without the separation. In health the separation was between the commissioning role of health authorities and the provider role of trusts. What has created the difficulty in this structure is the position of primary health care and in particular the role of GPs. They are both providers in their surgeries of care and also have a commissioning role which was explicitly given to them through the development of GP fund-holding.

In its elegant solution to the political commitment to abolish GP fund-holding, the government created primary care groups to retain the GP input into the commissioning of health care. These are now transmuting into primary care trusts but with the GP role firmly entrenched through the Executive's day-to-day input into the decision-making processes of the trust. The trusts not only are responsible for the quality of the delivery of primary health care but also are the commissioners of acute health care.

Notwithstanding the emerging rapprochement with the private sector, the room for manoeuvre in commissioning health care is limited. Patients want local services. Most patients are elderly and the idea of getting a hip replacement tomorrow 250 miles away from family and friends is unattractive. Contracts with acute hospitals are therefore block contracts with quality and performance standards attached. Occasionally cost and volume contracts may be negotiated with smaller specialist providers, but in terms of expenditure the block contracts are dominant. Dropping a contract with the local acute hospital is not a practical option as there is no over-supply in the market. Health care commissioning has therefore been focused on cost containment and in performance improvement in terms of length of stay, bed utilization and more recently on surgical outcomes. The Bristol child heart surgery inquiry may make a watershed in shifting the hands-off approach of commissioners on clinical issues.

Social care commissioning is, however, very different in its context. It requires a strategic sense of direction; it requires stakeholder commitment; and it requires the involvement of users and carers at all levels of the process. It is more competitive than the market in health care. It may require the stimulation of a market with a deliberate policy of assistance to bring more providers into play. It has no areas where the provider is beyond the scope of inspection and regulation which may extend to the nature of the management structure, financial controls and staffing ratios. This micro-management is foreign to health care commissioning. The extensive liaison with the voluntary sector as a major provider of social care is also relatively under-developed in health care commissioning with the exception of palliative care. The different skills required are considered below.

Shared values

Shared values have helped to make a success of community care. The values are essentially those of social work which was the leading profession in the development of social care. They assert the worth of each individual and their right to self-fulfilment. The status of social work as a true profession has been questioned and the BASW Code of Ethics skirts delicately around this by saying

> while social workers are accountable to those under whose authority they work, and responsible for the efficient performance of their professional task and for the management of the organization's resources, their primary responsibility is to those for whom they work, clients, groups, communities.

In addition to sections on anti-discriminatory practice and confidentiality, the Code says:

> they will help their clients, both individually and collectively to increase the range of choices open to them and their powers to make decisions, securing the participation, wherever possible, of clients in defining and obtaining services appropriate to their needs.
>
> (BASW 1996)

The emphases in this value statement are participation, self-determination and empowerment. They emphasize the social planning responsibilities of practice and locate individuals in the context of the families, groups and communities in which they live. They do not sit comfortably with the tradition of medicine firmly rooted in individual assessment, diagnosis and treatment with the doctor–patient relationship at the centre of professional responsibility.

The NHS Plan sometimes uses the language of social care values: 'the NHS will shape its services around the needs and preferences of individual patients, their families and carers . . . patients will have a greater say in the NHS, and the provision of services will be centred on patients' needs' (NHS Plan 2000: 4). 'A system designed around patients is a system with more power for patients' (ibid.: 15). 'Giving patients more powers in the NHS is one of the keys to unlocking patient-centred services' (ibid.: 30).

The proposals to achieve this include better information, strengthened patient choice, a new patient advocacy service, strengthened complaints procedure and an Annual National Patients survey which will have an impact on financial allocations. It is an impressive set of measures but as the section on delayed discharges made clear, choice and efficiency are not natural bedfellows. Which will have primacy when they are in conflict?

ACTIVITY 8.1: RECONCILING COMPETING VALUES

You are the commissioner for disability services in a new Care Trust. An additional £200,000 has been made available for disability services in the Service and Financial Framework plan. The trust has good clinical services for people with disabilities under the leadership of a gifted consultant. There is a small but vocal user group which has been highly critical of the lack of community support services, the limited funding for personal assistants and the scarcity of suitable accommodation for people in a wheelchair. As commissioner you have been negotiating with the housing authority who are willing to provide eight units providing that you contribute £150,000 to the purchase of specialist equipment and provide two care staff to support the new development. The user group supports the specialist equipment but vigorously opposes any care staff claiming the budget for personal assistants employed through direct payments should be increased. The consultant wants a new Registrar post and a junior house officer to free him to undertake research. This has been supported through the medical staffing committee as a priority.

How would you set about reconciling these competing claims? What values would be important to you in decision-making?

A NEW SET OF SKILLS

Bigger does not always mean better. As the exercise suggested, the advent of Care Trusts will create a new set of problems for commissioners. The skills required for commissioning were discussed in Chapter 2 but the complexity of the task means that others will need to be added to steer a path through the troubled waters of integrated care.

These will include:

- understanding the politics and pressures within the organization
- negotiating with professional interest groups concerned to protect their position
- developing a clear strategy and holding to it
- flexibility about the means to achieve the strategy including willingness to compromise

Understanding politics and pressures is always important. Political skills were identified earlier in understanding who are the key councillors and ensuring that their confidence is secured and maintained. The power structure within Care Trusts will be much more difficult to discern. It will almost certainly be located outside the Trust Board although the Board will be important. It may be a body analogous to the Primary Care Trust Executive which gives medical staff a formal position of influence or it may be mediated through pressures on the Chief Executive.

Securing a clear understanding about the committees, advisory groups, key individuals and stakeholder groups where support must be obtained for proposals, getting proposals in the form most likely to be acceptable to those bodies and ensuring that there is someone willing to articulate and support your case at the crucial meeting are essential.

What differentiates health and social care is the intensity of the inter-professional rivalries within health, the proliferation of the advisory mechanisms, the sophistication in understanding power relationships and the vigour with which conflicts are fought. Understanding how decisions are reached is therefore critical for successful commissioning.

Negotiation is an important skill in any commissioning role. In Care Trusts with their emphasis on inter-professional working it will be even more so. The best example of inter-professional working within the current delivery of health and social care can be found in community teams. These are the preferred delivery route for care for people with learning disabilities and mental health problems, may also be found in drug and alcohol services, and are clearly preferred in the NHS Plan as the best way to deliver community support services for older people.

What is evident, however, is the variability of such teams in their composition, their accountability arrangements, and their ability to blur professional boundaries. The word team is applied to teams where the professional disciplines hold rigidly to their area of specialist expertise but share the same office and contribute to shared case discussions, to teams where for various reasons a key member – usually a psychologist or psychiatrist – is located outside the team but attends for some team meetings, and for fully integrated teams where workers bring their skills to bear regardless of their previous background identifying themselves as a team member rather than nurse, psychologist or social worker.

Similar issues are found in accountability where ideally the team leader would have overall professional and managerial accountability and thus be able to hold staff to account for any failure of professional skill. In many teams, however, this has proved a step too far for the professions involved and a hybrid exists where managerial and professional accountability are split. In this arrangement a nurse in a team may be accountable to the psychologist team leader for how work is organized and programmed, for timekeeping and personnel issues but accountable to a senior nurse outside the team for professional supervision and evaluation.

The teamwork required for the effective operation of these teams has produced a burgeoning literature. Otreveit has written extensively on the skills needed to deliver a successful team and the different types of teams. He identifies four different models:

- a team with a single manager responsible for all the professions within the team
- a team co-ordinator with staff getting professional supervision from their respective professional lines
- a team manager buying in services which are managed by their respective professional lines
- a hybrid management structure with core staff directly managed, some services bought under contract and some jointly managed with a third party.

(Otreveit 1997: 28–31)

The role boundaries between the professions in a team are the third area where inter-professional tensions may be found. Inevitably in teams personal rivalries and tensions can be expressed in professional terms. The ambiguity about the boundaries of competence for nurses and social workers makes this particularly difficult if a social worker claims work on family relationships as their exclusive territory or a nurse claims unique skills in assessing the impact of physical ill-health on family functioning. The most successful teams seem to be those where no specific claims are made for professional expertise but where team members recognize that certain individuals possess special skills which would be very helpful in work with a particular client.

The commissioner has therefore to be clear about the type of team which they wish to see, clear about the accountability issue and sensitive to potential difficulties.

Developing a clear strategy is essential. This should be based on shared values, an agreed vision of the future and the major changes in policy and practice required to achieve that vision. This is likely to be the source of some difficulties for Care Trusts even where they are established by agreement between the health authority and the local authority.

Mental health services are likely to be those where most rapid progress is made in the achievement of integrated trusts linking commissioning and providing responsibilities. They are also the service area where there is a fast developing user movement deeply hostile to much current psychiatric practice. It has adopted the label of 'survivors of the mental health system' to encapsulate its view that the current system is often actively damaging to users. This poses a major task for the commissioner seeking to achieve an agreed view of the way forward!

In addition to the user interest, there is scope for confusion and duplication in the new roles in mental health services identified in the NHS Plan. These include:

- 1000 graduate primary care staff trained in brief therapy to support GPs
- 50 early intervention teams to support young people with psychosis and their families
- 335 crisis resolution teams
- 50 additional assertive outreach teams
- women-only day centres in every health authority
- 400 additional staff to support patients discharged from high security hospitals

It is far from clear whether community mental health teams as now constituted can withstand this fragmentation of different styles of intervention. It is not clear where the skills to staff these teams are to be found. And the varying numbers of teams suggest that some will be based on health authority boundaries, some on local authority boundaries and some will span more than one health authority, presenting great problems of coordination and communication. Yet all these teams have to be included as stakeholders in developing a service vision and values.

An intensive consultation exercise will be necessary to distil an agreed vision but the potential for fragmentation makes it all the more imperative that such a view is reached. Skilled external facilitation can be useful in opening up the conflict issues and helping to resolve them. But it will take time when there is external pressure from government and the Care Trust Board for quick results. Yet without that investment of time the result may be disastrous in a service where failures in communication and understanding have figured in too many inquiry reports into mental health-related deaths.

Flexibility is an undervalued virtue in commissioning. Knowing where you are going and how to get there are essential attributes but they can sometimes be associated with a single-mindedness of purpose which actually detracts from the achievement of the objective. Negotiating skills are about giving something to other people to secure their support. The best negotiations have an element of quid pro quo in which both parties get something they value from the agreement.

That requires flexibility. But the commissioner has to be clear about the areas where compromise is possible and those areas of the strategy which are non-negotiable. In a mental health strategy where resources are predicated on the closure of a long-stay psychiatric hospital and the redeployment of the resources released to develop community services, compromise could be possible on everything except the strategy of closure. The proposed date for closure could be negotiable; the terms of redundancy could be negotiable; the programme of retraining could be negotiable; travelling allowances could be negotiable; and another dozen issues offer room for flexibility in reaching agreement. Making use of that flexibility is often the key to sustaining morale during a time of change. The commissioner will, however, be aware that flexibility has a financial cost and the more is offered to the workforce, the less resources will be available for service development.

PERILS AND PITFALLS

In looking at the potential obstacles to change there are four obvious considerations which could slow or even derail the programme of change which is set out in the NHS Plan. These are:

- the impact of a general election on the legislative programme
- the slow pace of primary care trust development
- the reluctance of local government to delegate its powers
- supply difficulties in recruiting and retaining the additional staff anticipated

General elections can cause the loss of part of the government's legislative programme. Bills which are uncontentious are often rushed through in the last days of the Parliament prior to dissolution The process of the manifesto becomes critical in shaping the programme for the next years of government as manifestos set out a set of policy objectives and commitments across the spectrum of political activity. Manifestos and the subsequent election campaign then lead to a re-ordering of priorities.

At present after the economy and education, the NHS is high on the priority list. If the measures taken by the government result in visible improvements in the waiting lists, waiting times for treatment and intermediate care services, the political priority of the NHS will be reduced. The Department of Health had a hefty slice of the legislative programme between 1997 and 2001 and further measures of primary legislation could have to take a lower place in the programme.

Writing a plan is one thing, even one as infused with energy and drive as the NHS Plan. Securing its delivery may be another.

Primary care trusts are scheduled to be in existence throughout the country by 2004. That timetable is likely to be met but the pace of development will influence decisions about care trusts. PCTs have a huge agenda in developing primary health care and in commissioning acute health care. They may have a more secure financial base by virtue of the increased resources which have been made available but relative plenty can bring problems too. Business collapses rarely happen when there is tight restraint on company spending. Boo.com and the Dome are examples when expenditure was unrestrained and accompanied by wildly optimistic projections of revenue. The task of matching the increased resources to needs in a way to deliver positive outcomes will challenge the most effective PCT managers.

In this context one wonders how enthusiastic PCTs will be to extend their responsibility to Care Trusts in the short term.

Local government does not always do what central government wants. There is a residue of resentment in local government at the imposition of new structures sweeping away time-honoured committees. The rise of regulators from the Audit Commission, Best Value Inspectorate, OFSTED, Housing Inspectorate, Social Services Inspectorate, Joint Review teams and the National Care Standards Commission is viewed with a jaundiced eye. The reduction in control over education means that personal social services is one of the few direct services now controlled by local politicians.

In this context it is questionable whether there will be great enthusiasm for the delegation of powers to a Care Trust with it being viewed as a further erosion of local government responsibilities. The democratic deficit in the governance arrangements for trusts is likely to be a further area of concern with limited representation of elected members on the Trust Board. It is a very skilled and knowledgeable councillor who can argue successfully with full-time board members.

A further factor likely to make councillors reluctant to cede power and control is the part played by social services in the many inter-sectoral alliances in which local councils are involved. These include community safety partnerships, the Drug Action Team where local authority boundaries have replaced health authority boundaries as the geographical basis for the work, supported housing partnerships and regeneration initiatives where social services become involved in primary prevention.

Staffing is the unexpected issue which could derail the expected rapid progress to the NHS plan. Public service pay rates have fallen relative to the private sector in recent years and with low unemployment rates, difficulty in recruiting staff in nursing and social care is becoming acute. Some of the proposals envisage the appointment of new staff to improve services and others propose the creation of new occupational categories like the graduate primary mental health care workers.

The obvious response to recruitment problems is to increase pay levels but the NHS is a cash-limited service and any improvements will come at the cost of enhanced services to users. This will be a difficult judgement for the government but one which constitutes a real threat to the vision.

COMMISSIONING IN 2005

The purpose of this chapter is to examine the way in which commissioning is likely to change in the next few years so that the impact on those currently employed in commissioning roles and those moving into commissioning roles can be assessed.

The drivers for change and some of the potential obstacles have been identified. Prophecy is a dangerous activity in a field where so much change is anticipated. The views set out below may well be rendered redundant by events. Macmillan's famous caution to politicians of all parties about what might go wrong: 'events, dear boy, events', is true in this context as well. Scandal is a powerful driver of change. Evidence of social services failures or a primary care disaster in a PCT could change the pace and the direction of change.

A realistic assessment of the shape of social care services in 2005 would be one of messiness. Social care will be commissioned by a variety of public sector bodies. Social care could be commissioned by:

- Care Trusts serving a geographical area, probably a local authority boundary.
- Care Trusts serving a specific client group in a larger geographical area.
- Primary care trusts.
- Partnership Boards established to commission joint health and social care for a specific client group.
- Local partnerships to deliver a specific service, for example, Surestart programmes
- Social services departments.
- Other local authority-based configurations, for example, a joint education and social services department.
- National bodies like the National Treatment Agency for drug services.

Social services are likely to remain the primary commissioners of services for children although this may be by default in the absence of any other organization seeking to do so. Adult care will, however, be fragmented with different patterns dependent on the nature of health and social care relationships in the area, and the views of local councillors about the moves to greater partnership working.

Such messiness will cause duplication and lack of co-ordination. It will be difficult to come to an evidence-based decision about which model works best because of shifts in configuration of services. But one confident prediction can be made – the election manifestos of 2005 will set out proposals to end the confusion!

The voluntary sector and the private sector will continue to grow in responsibility as deliverers of social care as Best Value reviews expose the scale of overhead costs borne by services. The commissioner will be able to choose between competing private sector providers as the market becomes more mature.

However messy the picture may be, it is clear that links with health care will grow in importance. The task for commissioners from a social care background will be to ensure that the values of care in a social environment are retained, and that the emphasis on users and carers does not fall prey to inter-professional conflicts and power struggles.

KEY POINTS

☐ Care Trusts are the preferred choice of the government for delivering integrated care.

☐ The proposal is based on the presumed benefits of structural integration.

☐ Joint commissioners face huge challenges in delivering truly integrated care.

☐ Social care values of user empowerment may struggle in the new environment.

☐ Messiness rather than simplicity is likely to characterize commissioning arrangements in 2005.

KEY READING

The nature of this chapter looking ahead means that there is no book at present which deals with the topic. There are, however, two contemporary commentators on health and social care issues whose articles are invariably thought-provoking. Watch out for articles by Bob Hudson and Gerald Wistow as the government's intentions become clear.

CHAPTER 9

ACTIVITIES
Pointers to the issues

None of the approaches set out below are the only way to tackle the activities. You should, however, review your answer against the responses to the activities and some of the case studies below and assess whether there are any points which you have omitted to cover.

ACTIVITY 1.1 FACTORS DRIVING CHANGE

The share of personal social services delivered through the independent sector has increased because of:

- the rapid expansion of private residential care in the 1980s helped by no limit on social security funding
- a policy bias to a mixed economy
- the mistrust by governments of both parties of the public sector as an efficient provider

This trend is likely to continue because the last two factors listed above remain valid. The pressures from performance assessment and Best Value will put pressure on directly provided services.

ACTIVITY 1.2 WORKING WITH PROVIDERS

The voluntary group will score highly on values and knowledge of the local market as will the group of home care workers. Understanding of costs is less certain for the voluntary provider and may be a real difficulty for the group of home care staff because of their limited knowledge of overheads. By contrast, the residential care provider moving into a new business area may have less knowledge of the domiciliary care market but a better understanding of costs. Its value base would need to be tested. It would be improper for the commissioner to provide direct assistance to the possible in-house bid but quite appropriate to advise the group of legal and financial staff whom they could contact. Discussions with the potential providers have to be even-handed but will wish to explore in detail their understanding of the task and capacity to deliver a good service.

ACTIVITY 2.1 WRITING A STRATEGIC PLAN

A draft strategic commissioning statement for older people would need to:

- set out the arguments for change including uneven distribution of care, the cost of upgrading the residential homes, the alternative options for care, messages from research
- set out a timetable over five years to redistribute resources across localities so that no locality lost too much of its resources in one year (4 per cent is suggested)
- set out a timescale for formal consultation with service users and local community groups on individual home closures
- state the financial consequences and estimated real savings from closure and the strategy for reinvestment in alternative provision
- propose the ringfencing of resources freed up by closure until the true cost of alternative provision was clear

ACTIVITY 2.2 JOINT COMMISSIONING

As joint commissioner for disability services, your first task would be to:

- establish close working relationships with the user group to reassure them
- review the effectiveness of current resource utilization and form a view about whether value for money was being obtained
- if it is not, initiate a Best Value review to build a consensus for change and identify shortcomings
- propose options to the Partnership board for pooling budgets with a subcommittee of the Board acting as the management group for the pooled budget (i.e. get the politicians on your side!)

ACTIVITY 3.1 MINIMIZING RISK

The danger with the Senior Citizens Consultative Group is that councillors will be angered if they find out that these discussions are taking place without their knowledge. At least the chairman and arguably other councillors should be advised in advance to minimize any risk. The basis for the discussion which is exploratory at this stage also needs to be spelt out to the group. Even so, it would be prudent to have a contingency plan in case the information leaks to the press in a distorted form.

ACTIVITY 3.2 PROMOTING USER INVOLVEMENT

The suggested strategy to get greater user involvement needs to start with existing resources using Mencap and the two service users as the basis for establishing an effective user group. The Director and Head of Service can then be invited to a formal meeting to hear some of the concerns expressed directly. This might then constitute the basis for a separate day centre or a direct payments scheme if there is support for these initiatives from a wider grouping. Resident groups in the hostels and group homes should be established as a forum with a view to pushing provision towards the right-hand of the consultation to decision-making spectrum.

Inevitably there will be problems with some staff unused to this level of user involvement. The key to shifting the culture of a home or a department is to find champions of change, individuals able to embrace new methods of working and to enthuse others. After some initial shifts a user involvement strategy could be developed with targets against which progress could be measured.

ACTIVITY 4.1 PREPARING A CARE PLAN

The care plan for Mr and Mrs A needs clearly to separate their different needs. For Mr A the priority is to establish whether Mr A continues to want to care for his wife, and to persuade him to see respite care as a means of allowing him to continue to care not as a failure. The doctor and Mr A's daughter are potential allies in that process. If Mr A can be persuaded to use respite care, it will need careful introduction. Close liaison with the doctor will be necessary to see if any change in medication would relieve the more extreme symptoms of Alzheimer's.

Securing effective respite either in a residential setting or through a respite at home service, which might be more acceptable to Mr A, are the objectives but the real success measure is getting better support for Mr A.

ACTIVITY 5.1 DESKTOP EXERCISE

The desktop exercise would lead to:

*   a block contract for catering. It would be possible to parcel a series of separate contracts on a geographical basis
*   an individually tailored care package would require spot purchasing of the night sitting service, and individual negotiations with the day centre and an extension to the domiciliary care provider on a cost and volume basis
*   adjustment to the service specification for meals on wheels to ensure that ethnic-sensitive service is provided as a variation on the block contract, or spot purchasing from local restaurants serving Halal food

ACTIVITY 5.2 CHOOSING THE RIGHT AGREEMENT

The voluntary mental health organization could be the subject either of a contract or service agreement. Given the uncertainties about alternative funding, a contract might better formalize the position and set a limit to the authority's financial commitment. The performance standards would include numbers of café users, turnover and numbers of people moving from the café into employment settings as well as the level of support and supervision provided in the café.

ACTIVITY 6.1 COST AND QUALITY

Trading cost and quality is always difficult. Here a premium of £15 per week is the price payable for higher standards and greater flexibility. While a decision would be contingent on the assessment of the market trends in terms of supply, the upward pressure on prices makes the offer from the local home proprietor an attractive proposition especially as no guarantee of take-up is required.

ACTIVITY 6.2 LOOKING AT TENDERS

The questions to be put to the three tenderers are as follows:

Tender A

- How would the day-to-day management operate with a single manager for the three homes?
- Have you considered the implications of TUPE (Transfer of Undertaking Protection of Employees) Regulations in calculating staff savings?
- How detailed are the calculations on the 10 per cent savings on supplies and services?
- What is included in the 10 per cent overhead charge?
- What training programme is there for staff?
- What internal quality assurance measures does the organization use in managing other homes?

Tender B

- Does anybody in the consortium have experience of managing contracts?
- Does the consortium envisage any changes in the regime of the three homes?
- Other than loyalty to the existing staff, why is the consortium interested?
- What guarantee can it offer against business failure?
- If staff costs increase by more than RPI, how will the consortium cut costs?
- Has the consortium the capacity to deliver personnel services and financial control after stripping out bureaucracy and council overheads?
- Has the consortium a policy on staff training and development?

Tender C

- What experience does the housing provider have of learning disabilities?
- What staff support will be available for residents?
- The disposal of the Victorian home will be a capital receipt for the Council. Is that clearly understood?
- Have the implications of Supporting People for future funding been considered?
- Are the changes in conditions compatible with TUPE? What is the timescale for the anticipated savings?
- How will the overhead savings be made?
- What are the reasons for the high food costs?
- What quality assurance measures does the organization have?
- What staff training and development policies?

Areas of savings to be explored further are: with A – the proposed additional expenditure on day services; with B – changes in the pattern of staff or activities; with C – the higher spend on food and the TV chef!

ACTIVITY 7.1 OUTCOME MEASURES

Outcome measures for the drug rehabilitation centre:

- percentage completing treatment programme
- percentage clean after six months
- percentage clean after twelve months

Targets of 60 per cent, 40 per cent and 30 per cent would represent a good performance in this difficult area.

Outcome measures for the intensive domiciliary care:

- percentage receiving first visit within twelve hours of discharge
- percentage receiving seven-day-a-week service
- percentage receiving more than fifteen-hours-a-week service
- percentage readmitted to hospital within four weeks

Outcome measures for the adoption service:

- percentage of looked after children placed for adoption
- percentage of placements resulting in adoption
- percentage of adoption breakdown
- length of time between placement and adoption

ACTIVITY 7.2 QUALITY STANDARDS

As lead purchaser for drug and alcohol services, your initial focus will be on the development of a satisfactory alcohol service. You might therefore follow up direct contacts with the two known potential providers by a conference to which you would invite those providers together with other nationally known providers, local medical staff specializing in alcohol problems and voluntary organizations, both local and national, involved in alcohol issues. The purpose would be to review available evidence about the incidence of the problem, to share information about local resources and to pool ideas about gaps in service provision. This should provide the data on which to formulate a request for proposals setting out the anticipated level of resources available.

The standards which you would set out in that statement would include:

- numbers of clients expected to be seen
- availability and accessibility of the service
- percentage completing treatment programmes
- percentage dry or significantly reducing alcohol consumption at end of programme
- percentage dry or reduced consumption at six months follow-up

You may wish to use QUADS, *Quality in Alcohol and Drug Services* (1998) as the basis for quality standards to be applied.

ACTIVITY 7.3 QUALITY MEASURES IN CONTRACTS

Looking for quality in mental health services is a complex task. A systematic approach to quality would cover processes such as: access arrangements for contact, links to community services, ethnic sensitivity, internal quality assurance procedures. It would cover inputs: staffing support, training and development of staff, resources available to support staff. It would cover outcomes in terms of numbers remaining in community without further hospitalization and numbers moving into employment or New Deal programmes.

How best to package these requirements may vary according to the size and experience of the organization which wins the contract for the service, but a preliminary sort might insert:

- in the contract, levels of staffing, anti-discriminatory commitments, regular monitoring commitments and the data to be collected, accessibility arrangements, training and quality assurance
- in performance monitoring, numbers of people supported and numbers remaining in community and those proceeding into some form of employment, but in the annual performance review to include links with community services
- in codes of practice, compliance with national service framework where not specifically identified in contract or performance monitoring

ACTIVITY 8.1 RECONCILING COMPETING VALUES

Pragmatism has to govern the reconciliation of competing priorities. The primacy of users means that the development of supported housing has to take priority, but two pieces of negotiation are likely. First, if the housing authority insists on local authority care staff, that will have to be explained to users as a precondition of securing enhanced services. But the housing authority may be content if there are supporters available so this has to be explored first. Second, the consultant needs to be encouraged to take a broad view of services with an enhancement of clinical and research services being necessarily subordinate to direct services. There may be ways of sweetening this pill by a joint application for research funding to an external funder which might finance a research assistant.

CASE STUDY 8: DIRECT PAYMENTS

John should be considered for direct payments if that is his wish. It is consistent with his overall approach to life. The issue then becomes how best his decision-making can be supported. Here the specialist staff with whom John works are a crucial resource in being able to structure a scheme relevant to John's situation. The main obstacles are likely to come from councillors feeling that John should be helped by public services, staff concerned about his ability to manage direct payments and neighbours feeling that someone with John's level of disability should have a named social worker contact.

CASE STUDY 11: DECIDING ON EXTENSIONS

There is a clear case for extending the contract given the uncertainty about future needs. Arguments to be used would include the likelihood of increased use of contracts with the independent sector, the advantages of block contracting and the scope to renegotiate the terms of the contract when the authority's needs were clear.

BIBLIOGRAPHY

Audit Commission (1986) *Making a Reality of Community Care*, London: HMSO.

Audit Commission (1996) *Just Capital*, London: HMSO.

Audit Commission (1997) *Take Your Choice*, London: HMSO.

Audit Commission (2000) *Charging with Care*, London: HMSO.

Baldwin, M. (2000) *Care Management and Community Care*, Aldershot: Ashgate.

Bamford, T. (1990) *The Future of Social Work*, Basingstoke: Macmillan.

Banks, P. (1997) 'Making a positive impact for carers', *Care Plan*, vol. 3, no. 3, p. 23.

Barclay Report (1982) *Social Workers: Their Role and Tasks*, London: Bedford Square Press.

Bean, J. and Hussey, L. (1996a) *Managing the Devolved Budget*, London: HB Publications.

Bean, J. and Hussey, L. (1996b) *Costing and Pricing Public Sector Services*, London: HB Publications.

Bean, J. and Hussey, L. (1997) *Finance for Non-financial Public Sector Managers*, London: HB Publications.

British Association of Social Workers (1996) *Code of Ethics*, Birmingham: BASW.

Byford, S. (2000) 'Cost effectiveness and independent living', unpublished paper for Joseph Rowntree Foundation seminar.

Cassam, E. and Gupta, H. (1992) *Quality Assurance in Social Care Agencies*, Harlow: Longman.

Challis, D., Chesterman, J., Darton, R. and Traske, K. (1993) 'Case management in the care of the aged', in J. Bornat, C. Pereira, D. Pilgrim and F. Williams (eds) *Community Care: A Reader*, Basingstoke: Macmillan.

Community Care (2000a) 'Care home owners warn Hutton', 2–8 November.

Community Care (2000b) 'Direct payments gain popularity', 19 October, p. 5.

Community Care (2000c) 'Hutton sets the pace but can workers keep up?', 9–15 November, pp. 10–11.

Connor, A. and Black, S. (1994) *Performance Review and Quality in Social Care*, London: Jessica Kingsley.

Corrigan, P., Hayes, M. and Joyce, P. (1999) *Managing in the New Local Government*, London: Kogan Page.

Davies, B. (1992) *Care Management, Equity and Efficiency*, Canterbury: Personal Social Services Research Unit.

Davies, B., Bebbington, A. and Charnley, H. (1990) *Resources, Needs and Outcomes in Community-based Care*, Personal Social Services Research Unit, London: Gower.

Davies, B. and Challis, D. (1986) *Matching Resources to Needs in Community Care*, Aldershot: Gower.

Deakin, S. and Michie, J. (1997) *Contracts, Cooperation and Competition*, Oxford: Oxford University Press.

Department of the Environment, Transport and the Regions (2000) *Supporting People: Guidance*, London: DETR.

Department of Health (1989) *Caring for People: Community Care in the Next Decade and Beyond*, London: HMSO.

Department of Health (1995a) *An Introduction to Joint Commissioning*, London: Department of Health.

Department of Health (1995b) *Practical Guidance on Joint Commissioning for Project Leaders*, London: Department of Health.

Department of Health (1998) *Partnership in Action*, London: HMSO.

Department of Health (1999) *The Personal Social Services Performance Assessment Framework*, LASSL (99) 24, London: Department of Health.

Department of Health (2000a) *No Secrets*, Consultation Paper, London: Department of Health.

Department of Health (2000b) *Implementation of Health Act: Partnership Arrangements*, Health Service Circular 2000/10, LAC, London: Department of Health.

Douglas, A. and Philpot, T. (1998) *Caring and Coping*, London: Routledge.

Ellis, R. and Whittington, D. (1998) *Quality Assurance in Social Care*, London: Arnold.

Evers, A. *et al.* (eds) (1997) *Developing Quality in Personal Social Services*, Aldershot: Ashgate.

Flynn, N. (1997) *Public Sector Management*, Hemel Hempstead: Prentice-Hall.

Flynn, N. and Hurley, D. (1994) *Contracting in the Community Care Market*, Brighton: Pavilion.

Fowler, N. (1984) Speech to Joint Social Services Annual Conference, 27 September 1984.

Gilbert, N. (1983) *Capitalism and the Welfare State*, New Haven, CT: Yale University Press.

Goffman, E. (1962) *Asylums: Essays on the Social Situation of Mental Patients and Other Inmates*, New York: Doubleday.

Glendinning, C., Halliwell, S., Jacobs, S., Rummery, K. and Tyrer, J. (2000) *Buying Independence*, Bristol: Policy Press.

Griffiths Report (1988) *Community Care: Agenda for Action*, London: HMSO.

Gutch, R. (1992) *Contracting: Lessons from the USA*, London: National Council for Voluntary Organisations.

Harding, T. and Phillips, J. (1996) 'Providing long-term care through the market: experience in the USA', *Journal of Inter-Professional Care*, vol. 10, no. 1, pp. 33–41.

Hardy, B. and Wistow, G. (2000) 'Changes in the private sector', in B. Hudson (ed.) *The Changing Role of Social Care*, London: Jessica Kingsley.

Hill, M. (ed.) (2000) *Local Authority Social Services: An Introduction*, Oxford: Blackwell.

Hudson, B. (1994) *Making Sense of Markets in Health and Social Care*, Sunderland: Business Education Publishers.

Hudson, B. (ed.) (2000) *The Changing Role of Social Care*, London: Jessica Kingsley.

Ignatieff, M. (1989) *Political Quarterly*, Spring 1989.

Knapp, M. (ed.) (1995) *The Economic Evaluation of Mental Health Care*, University of Kent at Canterbury: PSSRU.

Knapp, M. and Forder, A. (1993) 'Purchasing dilemmas', *Community Care*, 2 December, p. 23.

Lapsley, I., Llewellyn, S. and Mitchell, F. (1994) *Management in the Public Sector*, Harlow: Longman.

Lawrie, A. (1994) *Managing Contracts*, London: Directory of Social Change and National Council for Voluntary Organisations.

Lewis, J. and Glennerster, H. (1996) *Implementing the New Community Care*, Buckingham: Open University Press.

Light, D. (1998) *Effective Commissioning*, London: Office of Health Economics.

Macadam, M. and Townsley, R. (1998) 'Who chooses', in L. Ward (ed.) *Innovations in Advocacy and Empowerment*, Chorley: Lisieux Hall.

McCoy, K. (2000), *Care in the Community*, Belfast: Department of Health and Social Services and Public Safety.

Maxwell, R. (1984) 'Quality assessment in health', *British Medical Journal* vol. 288, pp. 1470–2.

Means, R. and Smith, R. (1998) *Community Care*, Basingstoke: Macmillan.

Middleton, L. (1994) 'Little boxes are not enough', *Care Weekly*, vol. 306, January.

Middleton, L. (1999) 'Could do better . . .' *Professional Social Work*, November, pp. 8–9.

Morris, J. (1993) *Independent Lives: Community Care and Disabled People*, Basingstoke: Macmillan.

National Health Service Plan (2000) London: HMSO.

Neate, P. (2000) 'Hutton sets the pace but can workers keep up?' *Community Care*, 9–15 November, pp. 10–11.

Oliver, M. (1993) 'Disability, citizenship and empowerment', in The Disabling Society, *Workbook 2 for Course K665*, Milton Keynes: Open University Press.

Otreiveit, J. (1997) 'How to describe inter-professional working', in J. Otreivet, P. Matthias and T. Thompson (eds) *Inter-professional Working for Health and Social Care*, Basingstoke: Macmillan.

Perri 6 and Kendall, J. (1997) *The Contract Culture in Public Services*, Aldershot: Ashgate.

Pirsig, R. (1974) *Zen and the Art of Motor Cycle Maintenance* (1999 edition), London: Vintage.

QUADS (1998) *Quality in Alcohol and Drug Services*, London: DrugScope.

Rickford, F. (2000) 'Who is flying the plane?', *Community Care*, 19–25 October.

Rummery, K. and Glendinning, C. (2000) *Primary Care and Social Services: Developing New Partnerships for Older People*, Abingdon: Radcliffe.

Seebohm Report (1968) *Report of the Committee on Local Authority and Allied Personal Social Services*, London: HMSO.

Seed, P. and Kaye, G. (1994) *Handbook for Assessing and Managing Care in the Community*, London: Jessica Kingsley.

Simons, K. (1998) 'What really matters', in L. Ward (ed.) *Innovations in Advocacy and Empowerment*, Chorley: Lisieux Hall.

Simons, K. (1999) *A Seat at the Table: Involving People with Learning Difficulties in Purchasing and Commissioning Services*, Kidderminster: British Institute for Learning Disabilities.

Thornicroft, G. and Strathdee, G. (eds) (1996) *Commissioning Mental Health Services*, London: HMSO.

Titmuss, R. (1973) *The Gift Relationship*, London: Allen and Unwin .

Trevellion, S. (1999) *Networking and Community Partnerships*, Aldershot: Ashgate.

Wagner, G. (1988) *Residential Care: A Positive Choice. Report of the Independent Review of Residential Care*, London: HMSO.

Walker, A. and Warren, L. (1996) *Changing Services for Older People: The Neighbourhood Support Units Innovation*, Milton Keynes: Open University Press.

Walsh, K. (1995) *Public Services and Market Mechanisms*, Basingstoke: Macmillan.

Ward, L. (1998) *Innovations in Advocacy and Empowerment*, Chorley: Lisieux Hall.

Warner, N. (1992) *Choosing with Care*, London: HMSO.

Whittaker, A. 'Involving people with learning difficulties in meetings', in J. Bornat, C. Pereira, D. Pilgrim and F. Williams (eds) (1993) *Community Care: A Reader*, Basingstoke: Macmillan.

Williamson, H. (1997) 'How game theory makes the market manageable', *Care Plan*, vol. 3, no. 2, p. 13.

Wilson, J. (1998) *Financial Management for the Public Services*, Buckingham: Open University Press.

Wistow, G., Knapp, M., Hardy, B. and Allen, C. (1994) *Social Care in a Mixed Economy*, Buckingham: Open University Press.

Wistow, G., Knapp, M., Hardy, B., Forder, J., Kendall, J. and Manning, R. (1996) *Social Care Markets*, Buckingham: Open University Press.

INDEX